A Formal Feeling Comes

Poems in Form by Contemporary Women

Edited by Annie Finch

Story Line Press
1994

Published by Story Line Press, Inc., Three Oaks Farm, Brownsville, OR 97327

This publication was made possible thanks in part to the generous support of the Nicholas Roerich Museum, the Andrew W. Mellon Foundation, the National Endowment for the Arts and our individual contributors.

The author would like to thank the Graduate College of the University of Northern Iowa for a grant which helped complete this project; Alfred Dorn, Dana Gioia, R.S. Gwynn, Marilyn Hacker, Edward Hirsch, Molly Peacock, and Timothy Steele for help and invaluable suggestions; Story Line Press for believing in the project; Glen Brand, for his many creative contributions and his love and support; and, for their involvement and energy, the many poets who submitted poems and expressed interest in the book but couldn't be included in the final version.

Library of Congress Cataloging-in-Publication Data

A Formal feeling comes : poems in form by contemporary women / edited by Annie Finch.
     p.   cm.
    Includes bibliographical references and index.
    ISBN 0-934257-98-1 : $15.95
    1. American poetry—Women authors. 2. American poetry—20th century. 3. Literary form. 4. Women—Poetry. I. Finch, Annie, 1956– .
PS589.F67 1994   94-4906
811'.540809287—dc20   CIP

A Formal Feeling Comes

811.5408
FOR
1994

ACKNOWLEDGEMENTS

Grateful acknowledgement is given to the following publishers:

ELIZABETH ALEXANDER, "Kevin of the N.E. Crew," "Ladders,"
"House Party," "Who I Think You Are," *The Venus Hottentot*,
University of Virginia Press, 1990; JUDITH BARRINGTON, "Villanelle
IV," *History and Geography*, Eighth Mountain Press, 1989; ROSELLEN
BROWN, "Five Poems from *Cora Fry*," *Cora Fry*, Norton, 1977,
Unicorn Press, 1989; DEBRA BRUCE, "Two Couples," *The Kenyon
Review*; KELLY CHERRY, "The Bride of Quietness," *Lovers and
Agnostics*, Red Clay Books, 1975, "The Pines Without Peer," *Relativity:
A Point of View*, Louisiana State University Press, 1977, "His-
tory," "Reading, Dreaming, Hiding," "The Raiment We Put On,"
"History,"*God's Loud Hand*, Louisiana State University Press, 1993;
SANDRA CISNEROS, "Muddy Kid Comes Home," "The Poet
Reflects On Her Solitary Fate," *My Wicked Wicked Ways*, Third
Woman Press, 1987; CHERYL CLARKE, "What goes around comes
around," "The Change," *Living as a Lesbian*, Firebrand Books,
1986, "Tortoise and Badger," *Caprice*; CATHERINE DAVIS, "Out
of Work, Out of Touch, Out of Sorts," *North American Review*;
RITA DOVE, "Persephone Underground," and "History," *Grace
Notes*, Norton, 1989; SUZANNE J. DOYLE, "This Shade," "Some
Girls," "Hell to Pay," *Dangerous Beauties: Poems New and Selected*,
The Marjorie Cantor Press (Palo Alto, CA), 1992; ANNIE FINCH,
"A Reply from His Coy Mistress," *The Formalist*, "Dickinson,"
Poetry: An Introduction, Harper and Row, 1993; JOAN AUSTIN
GEIER, "On Your Twenty-First Birthday," *The Mother of Tribes*,
Four Circles Press, 1987; SARAH GORHAM, "Princess Parade,"
"The Empress Accepts the Head of a Teiping Rebel," *Sparrow*;
EMILY GROSHOLZ, "Eden," "Legacy," *Eden*, Johns Hopkins University
Press, 1992, "The Last of the Courtyard," *The River Painter*, Uni-
versity of Illinois Press, 1984; MARILYN HACKER, "Eight Days
in April," *Love, Death, and the Changing of the Seasons*, William
Morrow, 1986; "Ballad of Ladies Lost and Found," *Assumptions*,
Knopf, 1985; RACHEL HADAS, "The House Beside the Sea,"
PN Review; JOSEPHINE JACOBSEN, "Only Alice," *The Atlantic*;
LENORE KEESHIG-TOBIAS, "Mother With Child," *A Gathering
of Spirit*, Ed. Beth Brant, Sinister Wisdom Books, 1984; DOLORES
KENDRICK, "Solo: the good blues," "Gethsemane A.D.," "We
Are the Writing on the Wall," *Now is the Thing to Praise*, Lotus
Press (Detroit), 1984; JANE KENYON, "Travel: After a Death,"
"Inpatient," "Alone for a Week," *The Boat of Quiet Hours*, Graywolf,
1986; MARY KINZIE, "Ringing Words," *Summers of Vietnam*, Sheep
Meadow Press, 1990, "Sun and Moon," "Boy," "Sound Waves,"
"Canicula," *Autumn Eros*, Knopf, 1992; CAROLYN KIZER, "A
Muse of Water," excerpts from "Pro Femina," *Mermaids in the
Basement*,Copper Canyon Press, 1984; SYBIL KOLLAR, "Late Arrivals,"

Thirteenth Moon; MAXINE KUMIN, "Despair," *Our Ground Time Here Will be Brief*, Viking, 1982; PHILLIS LEVIN, "Dark Horse," "Citizens and Sky," *Temples and Fields*, University of Georgia Press, 1988; JANET LEWIS, "Time and Music," *Late Offerings*, Robert L. Barth, 1988; VASSAR MILLER, "How Far?," "Dirge in Jazz Time," "Light Reading," "Ecclesiastes the Second," *If I Had Wheels or Love: Collected Poems*, SMU Press, 1992; LESLIE MONSOUR, "A Dream of Dying," *Hellas*, "Emily's Words," *Gringuita Poems*, Missing Measures Press, 1990; HONOR MOORE, "First Time 1950," "A Green Place," *Memoir*, Chicory Blue Press, 1988; ELISE PASCHEN, "Litany," *Poetry*, "Confederacy," (originally titled, "Home for Heart"), *The Nation*; MOLLY PEACOCK, "ChrisEaster," "How I Had to Act," "Anger Sweetened," "Good Girl," "The Spell," *Take Heart*, Random House, 1989; HELEN PINKERTON, "On Dorothea Lange's Photograph 'Migrant Mother' (1936)," and "On Vermeer's 'Young Woman With a Water Jug' (1658) in the Metropolitan Museum," *The Harvesters and Other Poems on Works of Art*, R.L. Barth, 1984; MARY JO SALTER, "Chernobyl," "Rebirth of Venus," *Unfinished Painting*, Knopf, 1992, "What Do Women Want," *The New Yorker*; SONIA SANCHEZ, "Father and Daughter," *I've Been a Woman*, Third World Press, 1987, "Two Haiku," "Song No. 2," "Song No. 3," *Under a Soprano Sky*, Africa World Press, 1987; MAY SARTON, "The Tortured," *Writings on Writing*, Puckerbrush Press, 1989, *Collected Poems 1930–1993*, W.W. Norton, 1993; MAUREEN SEATON, "Fear of Subways," "Fear of Shoplifting," *Fear of Subways*, Eighth Mountain Press, 1990; ELIZABETH SPIRES, "The Comb and the Mirror," *Annonciade*, Viking Penguin, 1989; "A Little Song," *The Formalist*; MAURA STANTON, "Living Apart," *Tales of the Supernatural*, David R. Godine, 1988; PATRICIA STORACE, "Wedding Song," "The Archaeology of Divorce," "King Lear Bewildered," *Heredity*, Beacon Press, 1987; MONA VAN DUYN, "Out-of-Body Concentration," *Ecstatic Occasions, Expedient Forms*, ed. David Lehman, Macmillan, 1987, "Homework," *To See, To Take*, Atheneum 1970, "The Vision Test," *Letters for a Father and Other Poems*, Atheneum, 1982, "Sonnet for Minimalists," *Near Changes*, Knopf, 1990; MARILYN NELSON WANIEK, "Diverne's Waltz," "Chosen," "Balance," *The Homeplace*, Louisiana State University Press, 1990; MILDRED WESTON, "Primitive Place," "Departure," *The Green Dusk: Selected Poems*, Owl Creek Press, 1987; GAIL WHITE, "The Leopard in Eden," *Sibyl and Sphinx* (with Barbara Loots), Rockhill Press, 1988; CAROLYN BEARD WHITLOW, "Book of Routh," "Rockin' a Man, Stone Blind," "Poem for the Children," *Wild Meat*, Lost Roads Press, 1986; NANCY WILLARD, "The Ballad of Biddy Early," "The Cat's Second Song," "The Speckled Hen's Morning Song to Biddy Early," *The Ballad of Biddy Early*, Knopf, 1989; NELLIE WONG, "Grandmothers' Song," "Ironing," *Dreams in Harrison Railroad Park*, Kelsey Street Press, 1977.

*T*his book is dedicated to
Diane Middlebrook and Ntozake Shange

INTRODUCTION

"After great pain, a formal feeling comes—"
                                            —Emily Dickinson

A Formal Feeling Comes: Poems in Form by Contemporary Women reflects a surprising development in contemporary women's poetry in the United States: a widespread turn—or return—to "formal" poetics. Readers who have been following the discussion of the "New Formalism" over the last decade may not expect to find such a diversity of writers and themes in a book of formal poems; the poems collected here contradict the popular assumption that formal poetics correspond to reactionary politics and elitist aesthetics. This does not mean, however, that literary and cultural politics have not affected women's use of poetic form. For serious twentieth-century women poets, traditional poetic form is a troubled legacy. The lineage of women poets in English is largely a formal one, but since the Modernist period, many have had reason to be ambivalent about form.

Women poets found themselves in a double bind during the reign of Modernism, in spite of the fact that their predecessors—from Lydia Sigourney to Louise Imogen Guiney—had developed a popular mode of female poetry during the course of the nineteenth century. While a line of male poetic experimenters including Smart, Blake, Whitman and Hopkins inspired the modernist revolution for male poets, women's poetry had long tended to favor accessibility and community-building over radical innovation. Even Dickinson's innovative poems remain within traditional formal limits much more than those of, for example, her contemporary Whitman.

1

As one critic characterizes the female poet's predicament, "a modern woman poet could not be a woman poet without reaching for a tradition that would violate the unconventionality of modernism and seem politically regressive."[1] In the early twentieth century, the price of participation in the new movement was the repression or abandonment of the women's poetic tradition.

"Of sugar and spice and everything nice,/That is what bad poetry is made of," quipped William Carlos Williams in ironically perfect rhyme. Like other key modernist writers, Williams linked the major line of women's poetry with traditional verse form and with inferior writing. Ezra Pound is unlikely to have been thinking of formal verse when he declared, "poetry speaks phallic direction," and James Joyce meant to praise the metrically revolutionary *The Waste Land* when he observed that it "ends [the] idea of poetry for ladies." Elsewhere Pound remarked that he wanted "to write 'poetry' that a grown man could read without groans of ennui, or without having to have it cooed in his ear by a flapper."[2] Female modernists distanced themselves from the mode of more traditional women poets. Privately, H.D. is reported to have "considered herself and [Marianne] Moore far superior to other women poets such as Elinor Wylie, Edna St. Vincent Millay, or Sara Teasdale."[3]

Teasdale, Alice Dunbar-Nelson, Millay, Wylie, Louise Bogan and others carried on the mainstream tradition nonetheless, continuing to write in traditional forms even after the modernist revolt. Although by mid-century almost all of the women poets of the nineteenth and early twentieth centuries had fallen out of print— and most certainly out of fashion—the legacy would continue, haltingly and often in secret. While Sylvia Plath was determined not to "write simple lyrics like Millay," Anne Sexton and Tillie Olsen guiltily confessed to each other their private love for the work of Millay and Teasdale.[4]

The poets in this anthology are reclaiming a formal inheritance more openly than women have done in many decades, and their work demonstrates that the long tradition of women's formal poetry is evolving once again. When I began to collect the poems for this anthology, I had no idea of the variety and extent of formalism among women poets. These poems have been gathered from all over the poetic map. With the exception of Marilyn Hacker, whose direct influence can be seen in the work of a number of the poets included here, there has been no particular central model for a return to conspicuously formal poetry. Far from being a poetic movement in the usual senses, the kind of "New Formalism" represented in this book has had an almost unconscious, grass-roots development.

Since one of the aims of this collection is to emphasize the continuity of women's formal poetry, I have included several important early poems by contributors whose careers are long-established. In almost all of these cases, a more recent poem is published as well. I regret that some writers could not be included for various reasons.

Defining "formal" poetry broadly as poetry that foregrounds the artificial and rhetorical nature of poetic language by means of conspicuously repeated patterns, I have chosen a continuum of formal poems, from regular rhyme and meter through accentual verse through nonmetrical rhyming poems to repetitive chants. Each of the poems included here involves conspicuous repetition, of vowels and consonants (rhyme), rhythmic patterns (meter), phrases (refrain or anaphora) or larger poetic patterns (stanza form). Many of the poems also engage the traditions that have developed around these root-techniques in English-language poetry.

A reader not familiar with the techniques of prosody will benefit by reading this book in conjunction with a handbook of versification such as Miller Williams' *Patterns of Poetry*, Babette Deutsch's *Poetry Handbook*, or Lewis Turco's *Book of Forms*. *A Formal Feeling Comes* includes examples of the most important prosodic forms in English—iambic and triple meters in a variety of line lengths, both rhymed and unrhymed; various quatrain rhyme patterns including the Italian (abba) and English (abab); other stanza patterns such as the hymn stanza, terza rima, rhyme royal, and sapphic stanza; and forms such as the villanelle, sestina, ballade, Petrarchan and Shakespearean sonnet, crown of sonnets, blues, chant, haiku, and pantoum. I have also included several poems in original or "nonce" forms ranging from pun-poems to oral literature-based chants.[5] Appendix A describes the technique of each poem, and Appendix B groups poems according to form.

To obtain a sense of the range of contemporary women's approaches to form, readers will want to compare the various versions of a form such as, for example, the sonnet. Most women poets have shied away from the sonnet for decades, perhaps sensing that, as Rachel Blau Du Plessis puts it, "The sonnet is a genre already historically filled with voiceless, beautiful female figures in object position"—Millay and Barrett Browning notwithstanding.[6] Many of the poets here use the sonnet form as they have inherited it, sometimes with ironic subject matter, while others change its form: some poets keep rhyme without meter, and others use subtle or rearranged rhyme schemes that are easier to miss in their "sonnets." [7]

The contributors' statements on poetics, all but two (those by Sarton and Van Duyn) written especially for this book, provide clues about the reasons for these different approaches and the appeal of form for various poets. A number of contributors, sensitive to the gender implications of form, write in historically powerful poetic forms in order to transform them and claim some of their strength. Rita Dove, for example, describes her chosen form (the sonnet) as "stultifying," but hears voices in it that are "sing[ing] in their chains." Others, like Molly Peacock, find themselves freed, imaginatively or emotionally, by the aesthetic constraints of form which make feelings "safe to explore." Some relish the intellectual challenge of a rhyme scheme, while others describe the physical pleasure they experience among the rhythms of a metrical line and, like Carolyn Kizer, associate the beat of meter with the rhythms of the body. The passion for form unites these many and diverse poets. As Marilyn Hacker writes, "When I see a young (or not-so-young) writer counting syllables on her fingers, or marking stresses for a poem she's writing, or one she's reading, I'm pretty sure we'll have something in common, whatever our other differences may be."

As this book shows, women are taking on the risks of form in new ways. At their best, these poets combine the intellectual strength, emotional freedom, and self-knowledge women have gained during the twentieth century with the poetic discipline and technique that have long been the female poet's province. These poems point the way to a true linking of the strengths of the old with the strengths of the new: not a nostalgic return to the old forms but an unprecedented relationship with their infinite challenges.

NOTES

1. Suzanne Clark, "The Unwarranted Discourse: Sentimental Community, Modernist Women, and the Case of Millay," *Genre* 20: 2 (1987): 145.

2. Quoted in David Perkins, *A History of Modern Poetry* (Cambridge: Harvard UP, 1976) 298. The quotes from Joyce and Williams, and Pound's quote on phallic direction, are collected in Sandra M. Gilbert and Susan Gubar, *No Man's Land: The Place of the Woman Writer in the Twentieth Century, Vol. 1: The War of the Words* (New Haven: Yale UP, 1987) 155-56.

3. Barbara Guest, *Herself Defined: The Poet H.D. and Her World* (London: Collins, 1985) 133.

4. Plath is quoted in Gilbert and Gubar 204. The Sexton anecdote is in Diane Middlebrook, *Anne Sexton: A Biography* (Boston: Houghton Mifflin, 1991) 196.

5. I also urge those interested in chant forms to read the title poems from Joy Harjo's *She Had Some Horses* (Thunder's Mouth Press) and Pat Parker's *Movement in Black* (Eighth Mountain Press).

6. Rachel Blau DuPlessis, "Thinking About Annie Finch, On Female Power and the Sonnet," *(How)ever* VI: 3 (Summer 1991) 16.

7. The focus of this book does not include the work of several contemporary women poets who are using the sonnet as the basis for even more experimental work, engaging with the idea of the form more than with its technical aspects. Readers interested in pursuing this phenomenon should investigate in particular Bernadette Mayer's *Sonnets* (Tender Buttons) and Irene Klepfisz's "Work Sonnets with Notes and a Monologue About a Dialogue" from *A Few Words in the Mother Tongue* (Eighth Mountain Press).

A Formal Feeling Comes

ELIZABETH ALEXANDER
A MULTIPLICITY OF FORMS

"Form," per se, is what helps me organize my poems. It is a box or a vessel or an outline or a shape for the words to live within. When a teacher first told me that "poems will suggest their own shape to you," I didn't believe it, but I've mostly found it to be true: early on in the writing a line length or rhythm seems to govern, and I tend to shape the rest of the poem accordingly. The "weight" of the poem, its heft, also becomes pretty much clear as I work.

Form to me does not just mean European forms such as the sonnet. It also means forms suggested by the blues or jazz, soul music, call and response communal talk, vernacular speech. It's important to understand the logic to those shapes, as well, and to think about the various syntactic, rhythmic, and organizational logics available to writers who are listening and looking for a multiplicity of forms.

KEVIN OF THE N.E. CREW

From the bus I see graffiti:
"Kevin of the N.E. Crew."
These walls cave walls hieroglyphics—
Who am I sit next to you?

Turn your head, boy. Look at me, boy.
Dark day, sweet smell, smoke smell blue.
Split-lip black boy brain smell sweet boy,
Look my way, boy. Look at you.

Nine boys smoking angel weed
Saw a lady that they knew,
Dragged the lady in the alley,
What they do—

Don't look for an explanation
(Broken glass and foot-long pole)
"Baby Love," "Snot-Rag," "Lunchbox," "Chrissie"—
Cave walls heart walls silent hole

Who tongue bled imagination?
Who is know, boy? Who are you?
Hey girl. You girl. Look my way girl.
Look at me girl look at you.

Made them. Claim them. These nine black boys.
Bus stops. Off. Stops. Passing through.
Smoke   glass   cave   walls
    weed   fence   pole   split
Kevin

LADDERS

Filene's department store
near nineteen-fifty-three:
An Aunt Jemima floor
display. Red bandanna,

apron holding white rolls
of black fat fast against
the bubbling pancakes, bowls
and bowls of pale batter.

This is what Donna sees
across the "Cookwares" floor,
and hears, "Donessa?" *Please,
this can not be my aunt.*

Father's long-gone sister,
nineteen-fifty-three. "Girl?"
Had they lost her, missed her?
This is not the question.

This must not be my aunt.
Jemima? Pays the rent.
Family mirrors haunt
their own reflections.

Ladders. Sisters. Nieces.
As soon a live Jemima
as a buck-eyed rhesus
monkey. Girl? Answer me.

WHO I THINK YOU ARE

Empty out your pockets nighttime, Daddy.
Keys and pennies, pocket watch, a favored
photograph of Ma, and orange-flavored
sucker-candies, in the dresser caddy.

Grandpa leaves his silver in his trousers,
potions for catarrh set on the bureau,
and his Castile soap. "All Pure." Oh,
those oval, olive cakes for early rousers!

Baba's home is different from my daddy's:
the sofa arms are draped with quiet lace.
Does he fix fish with cardamon and mace?
Coupons in a cookie tin. Meat patties,

Steaming Cream of Wheat and ripe banana,
juice cups with the little paper hats,
the guava jelly jars on plastic mats.
We are your children and receive your manna.

I see you both. I see what's in your pockets.
Coins from you, Dad'. Baba? what's for me?
Fortune cookies, child, and sacks of tea,
cigar bands and glinting, dimestore lockets.

ZODIAC

You kissed me once and now I wait for more.
We're standing underneath a swollen tree.
A bridge troll waits to snatch me if I cross.
Your bicycle handles are rusted blue.

My mouth has lost its flavor from this kiss.
I taste of warm apple. My lips are fat.
If these blossoms fall they'll mark our faces:
Gold shards of pollen or flower-shaped dents.

Is it bird wings that bat between my legs?
Is there a myth for trolls? Bullfinch says no.
My mother has a friend who reads the stars.
I am fourteen. "My dear, you look in love."

Your fingers stained dull orange from the bike.
Svetlana eyes and hands, no crystal ball.
White ripe blossoms on a trembling tree.
Again, I think. *I want you to kiss me.*

NELL ALTIZER
A Different Spin

The "little song" of the sonnet—especially the Petrarchan one with its unbalanced architecture, its license to roam sensuously among rhymes, the sexy thud, thud, thud its final orchestration can bang out—is an especially apt room for the raw rage which often accompanies passion. The octave gives an illusion of space and luxuriance: whether the sounds link or accumulate there is in the closed and open bracelets of the scheme an overarching airiness which invites dalliance and risk. After that voluptuous stretch, the turn and fall into six lines where all must be resolved or revenged accelerates anxiety, tightens the musculature, thickens the beat. At the end of the sonnet there is something hot and unfinished, a pulsing nerve that is the fuse of the next, then the next in what may happily turn out to be a sequence.

These sonnets are part of a sequence of six, all beginning with an opening line of Hopkins' "Terrible Sonnets," and entitled (in a phrase also borrowed with a pronoun change from Hopkins) "Love Letters to Her Who Lives (Alas!) Away." Why a woman's love for a married woman should find resonance in a Jesuit priests's anguished cries to a disappeared God beats me. Those sonnets, which I have loved for decades, simply throbbed in my love-hungover head one dawn and banged away during the sixteen hours or so it took me to draft the first blueprint for the series. By introducing an aesthetic quandary—is Hopkins' passion secularized (perhaps vulgarly so) or is a woman's deviant obsession transfigured?—I hoped to foreground the tension a woman's pen always draws against canonical forms. All sonnet sequences reverberate with other sequences just as fugues recall fugues and odalisques other odalisques. Women catch these conventions with a different twist and pitch them back (past grief) with a different spin, which is what makes formal poetry by women so rigorous, so invigorating.

SONNET 2
(from "Love Letters to Her Who Lives [Alas!] Away")

My own heart let me have. More pity on
yours, too. Where is it? Pray you undo that button
that undid me in the motel room. Obsidian
unlatching to the nursery of sons,
those lotions in your satchel rubbing the skin
of my teeth, that neck disdaining and oblique
above the breaststone, breath so above the bite
that seeks the priming pump. Saint Valentine

was burned alive for this locating of the god.
Boys, girls, what did he care who got together?
A drop in the bucket of love, the machinery's
going: suck, gulp, swive, woman alive! Whose body
now is maul. I call. The record's on: "You have
    reached
the residence of Mr. and Mrs. Forever."

SONNET 5
(from "Love Letters to Her Who Lives [Alas!] Away")

No, I'll not, carrion, comfort you. Comfort
yourself. My heart's a little sweatshop, hundreds
of girls, some bleeding, sewing, bentback, biting
   thread
and treading. One dummy dreams of a ledean body,
   short
blonde, who will wear this dress under needle's
foot. She dreams of dancing, holding her. Plumeria
in the air, from the buffet, mouton cadet
beckons, silk whisk, the Tales of Hoffman on the
   fiddle

when like a vine of trillium the strap
she sewed falls, fetching from her partner's shoulder.
Failure, she thinks: the thread not knotted. Boss
man down in a minute with complaints, the job lost.
O, pretty pearl, lean here. I'll tuck the stitching back,
show you factories, milltowns, whorehouses, when
   you're older.

JULIA ALVAREZ
HOUSEKEEPING CAGES

Sometimes people ask me why I wrote a series of poems about housekeeping if I'm a feminist. Don't I want women to be liberated from the oppressive roles they were condemned to live? I don't see housekeeping that way. They were the crafts we women had, sewing, embroidering, cooking, spinning, sweeping, even the lowly dusting. And like Dylan Thomas said, we sang in our chains like the sea. Isn't it already thinking from the point of view of the oppressor to say to ourselves, what we did was nothing?

You use what you have, you learn to work the structure to create what you need. I don't feel that writing in traditional forms is giving up power, going over to the enemy. The word belongs to no one, the houses built of words belong to no one. We have to take them back from those who think they own them.

Sometimes I get in a mood. I tell myself I am taken over. I am writing under somebody else's thumb and tongue. See, English was not my first language. It was, in fact, a colonizing language to my Spanish Caribbean. But then Spanish was also a colonizer's language; after all, Spain colonized Quisqueya. There's no getting free. We are always writing in a form imposed on us. But then, I'm Scherezade in the Sultan's room. I use structures to survive and triumph! To say what's important to me as a woman and as a Latina.

I think of form as territory that has been colonized, but that you can free. See, I feel subversive in formal verse. A voice is going to inhabit that form that was barred from entering it before! That's what I tried in the "33" poems, to use my woman's voice in a sonnet as I would use it sitting in the kitchen with a close friend, talking womanstuff. In school, I was always trying to inhabit those forms as the male writers had. To pitch my voice to "Of man's first disobedience, and the fruit...." If it didn't hit the key of "Sing in me, Muse, and through me tell the story," how could it be important poetry? The only kind.

While I was in graduate school some of the women in the program started a Women's Writing Collective in Syracuse. We were musing each other into unknown writing territory. One woman advised me to listen to my own voice, deep inside, and put that down on paper. But what I heard when I listened were voices that said things like "Don't put so much salt on the lettuce, you'll wilt the salad!" I'd never heard that in a poem. So how could it be poetry? Then, with the "33" sonnet sequence, I said, I'm going to go in there and I'm going to sound like myself. I took on the whole kaboodle. I was going into form, sonnets no less. Wow.

What I wanted from the sonnet was the tradition that it offered as well as the structure. The sonnet tradition was one in which women were caged in golden cages of beloved, in perfumed gas chambers of stereotype. I wanted to go in that heavily mined and male labyrinth with the string of my own voice. I wanted to explore it and explode it too. I call my sonnets free verse sonnets. They have ten syllables per line, and the lines are in a loose iambic pentameter. But they are heavily enjambed and the rhymes are often slant-rhymes, and the rhyme scheme is peculiar to each sonnet. One friend read them and said, "I didn't know they were sonnets. They sounded like you talking!"

By learning to work the sonnet structure and yet remaining true to my own voice, I made myself at home in that form. When I was done with it, it was a totally different form from the one I learned in school. I have used other traditional forms. In my poem about sweeping, since you sweep with the broom and you dance—it's a coupling—I used rhyming couplets. I wrote a poem of advice mothers give to their daughters in a villanelle, because it's such a nagging form. But mostly the sonnet is the form I've worked with. It's the classic form in which we women were trapped, love objects, and I was trapped inside that voice and paradigm, and I wanted to work my way out of it.

My idea of traditional forms is that as women much of our heritage is trapped in them. But the cage can turn into a house if you housekeep it the right way. You housekeep it by working the words just so.

HOW I LEARNED TO SWEEP

My mother never taught me sweeping...
One afternoon she found me watching
t.v. She eyed the dusty floor
boldly, and put a broom before
me, and said she'd like to be able
to eat her dinner off that table,
and nodded at my feet, then left.
I knew right off what she expected
and went at it. I stepped and swept;
the t.v. blared the news; I kept
my mind on what I had to do,
until in minutes, I was through.
Her floor was as immaculate
as a just-washed dinner plate.

I waited for her to return
and turned to watch the President,
live from the White House, talk of war:
in the Far East our soldiers were
landing in their helicopters
into jungles their propellors
swept like weeds seen underwater
while perplexing shots were fired
from those beautiful green gardens
into which these dragonflies
filled with little men descended.
I got up and swept again
as they fell out of the sky.
I swept all the harder when
I watched a dozen of them die...
as if their dust fell through the screen
upon the floor I had just cleaned.
She came back and turned the dial;
the screen went dark. *That's beautiful,*
she said, and ran her clean hand through
my hair, and on, over the window-
sill, coffee table, rocker, desk,
and held it up—I held my breath—
that's beautiful, she said, impressed,
she hadn't found a speck of death.

NAMING THE FABRICS

Mother, unroll the bolts and name
the fabrics from which our clothing came,
dress the world in vocabulary:
broadcloth, corduroy, gingham, terry.

Gingham and calico, crepe and gauze,
gabardine, organdy, wool, madras,
fabrics, Mother, name them all,
jersey, chambray, satin, voile.

"Give me a yard of that dotted swiss,
satin to rein in my junior miss
with a crimson sash and a show-off bow,
for schoolclothes yards of calico.

"'Course I'd like some permanent press
with four daughters and a man to dress—
I've got them down to a set of numbers
though the girls keep inching out of their jumpers.

"I'd like a lick of that wedge of velvet—
rich as a bar of chocolate fudge.
I can see him through the sheer chiffon
sigh at the girls he sowed as sons.

"All the better! Four sets of hands
to puzzle the squares on a yard of lawn,
outline in chalk, then satin-stitch
the monograms on his handkerchiefs.

"Broadcloth, Herringbone, Oxford, Cheviot,
Seersucker, Duck: his suits are cut
from proud cloths whose names suggest
coats of arms and the shroud of conquest.

"My girls were cut out of different cloths—
my legs scissoring with love
(they're old enough to hear it said)
on the muslin sheets of the homemade bed.

"My eldest is jersey, a sensible fabric,
to make up for the second, a pretty dramatic
damask! The third is genuine kersey.
My baby, a finicky dimity.

"As for me, if I had to pick,
I'd be a reversible fabric,

on the worn-out side, a wife and mother,
a brand-new woman on the other!

"With wash-and-wear marquisette legs and feet,
organdy thighs, a thin tricot waist,
a chambray bodice and brocade breasts,
no-iron plisse for my face."

Mother, be made of marquisette,
brocade, plisse. And when your spirit
discards itself from the spindle spine,
may your clothes be hung on the washday line.

May the sleeves fill with windy limbs,
and the busts bulge with a sudden gust,
the hips indulge in the fattening wind,
and the snap of the breeze be the thump of the pulse.

Four sets of hands will tend to you.
For although your being has fallen through
the sieve of these fabrics, still you live
as the damp lap dries and the tight seams give

in the gingham, calico, crepe and gauze,
gabardine, organdy, wool, madras,
selves, Mother, you've worn them all:
jersey, chambray, satin, voile.

SONNET 1
(from "33")

Everything that happens to me these days
is dangerous with love. I'm a witch
at full moon. I can't be sure
of anyone. I stiffen if I'm grazed
by an arm or a hand combs through my hair.

I won't drink out of a strange cup or use
borrowed clothing. Everything is infused
with hazard and imagination's power,
stronger than actual. I won't accept
dinner invitations in case magic
powders have been disguised in the garlic
seasonings. But my house, though protected
with charms, can't block the spell mortality
has cast, thirty-two, I turn thirty-three.

SONNET 42
(from "33")

Sometimes the words are so close I am
more who I am when I'm down on paper
than anywhere else as if my life were
practising for the real me I become
unbuttoned from the anecdotal and
unnecessary and undressed down
to the figure of the poem, line by line,
the real text a child could understand.
Why do I get confused living it through?
Those of you, lost and yearning to be free,
who hear these words, take heart from me.
I once was in as many drafts as you.
But briefly, essentially, here I am...
Who touches this poem touches a woman.

BILINGUAL SESTINA

Some things I have to say aren't getting said
in this snowy, blonde, blue-eyed, gum chewing
   English,
dawn's early light sifting through the *persianas* closed
the night before by dark-skinned girls whose words

evoke *cama, aposento, sueños* in *nombres*
from that first word I can't translate from Spanish.

Gladys, Rosario, Altagracia—the sounds of Spanish
wash over me like warm island waters as I say
your soothing names: a child again learning the
    nombres
of things you point to in the world before English
turned *sol, tierra, cielo, luna* to vocabulary words—
sun, earth, sky, moon—language closed

like the touch-sensitive *morivivir* whose leaves closed
when we kids poked them, astonished. Even Spanish
failed us then when we realized how frail a word
is when faced with the thing it names. How saying
its name won't always summon up in Spanish or
    English
the full blown genii from the bottled *nombre*.

Gladys, I summon you back with your given *nombre*
to open up again the house of slatted windows closed
since childhood, where *palabras* left behind for English
stand dusty and awkward in neglected Spanish.
Rosario, muse of *el patio*, sing in me and through me
    say
that world again, begin first with those first words

you put in my mouth as you pointed to the world—
not Adam, not God, but a country girl numbering
the stars, the blades of grass, warming the sun by
    saying
el sol as the dawn's light fell through the closed
persianas from the gardens where you sang in Spanish,
Esta son las mañanitas, and listening, in bed, no English

yet in my head to confuse me with translations, no
    English

doubling the world with synonyms, no dizzying
   array of words,
—the world was simple and intact in Spanish
awash with *colores, luz, sueños,* as if the *nombres*
were the outer skin of things, as if words were so
   close
to the world one left a mist of breath on things by
   saying

their names, an intimacy I now yearn for in English—
words so close to what I meant that I almost hear my
   Spanish
blood beating, beating inside what I say *en inglés.*

JUDITH BARRINGTON
SCAFFOLDING

A few years ago, I wrote a sequence of six villanelles dealing with my mother's death by drowning. I do not think I could have written that particular piece without a strict form. The boundaries—the finite patterns that could not spill out into the unknown—provided a framework that I needed for the subject. I also think that the villanelle itself was important to the subject—I couldn't have used just any tight form. I had always thought that the shape of the villanelle, with its repeating lines that come together at the end, suggested both tides and circles. These poems were full of ocean, waves and moon.

Some critics equate traditional form with conservatism but for me some of my most radical work has emerged from between the scaffolding of a known form. Poets surely can say the same old things in any form—or in no form at all. New vision is rare enough. I welcome it whatever pattern it makes on my page.

VILLANELLE VI

When I stand on the shore, I wonder where you are
somewhere in that fathomed room behind
the waves like doors that slowly swing ajar.

Dappled stones at my feet are smeared with tar.
Sucked by the undertow, they jostle and grind
while I stand on the shore, wondering where you are.

Beyond the raging surf, beyond the bar,
in your green chamber you hide, forever blind
to the waves like doors that slowly swing ajar

inviting me in, enticing me from afar,
but their curling crests are an unmistakable sign
I should stay on shore and wonder where you are.

Your voice in the wind doesn't say where you are
and I listen less and less, resigned
to those waves like doors that slowly swing ajar.

Will the light of the crescent moon, the northern star
create a pathway we both can find
as I stand on the shore wondering where you are,
and the waves like doors slowly swing ajar?

ROSELLEN BROWN
On Syllabics and Cora Fry

No work exists in a vacuum. Every new work stands in a particular relationship to what has come before, either a whole career's-worth, or simply the piece that's just been completed. In the case of my book-length poem *Cora Fry*, two things had just happened to me when I wrote it. First, I had just survived months of reading poetry manuscripts for the contest of a university press and I was dismayed by the sameness I had been swamped by: competent, interchangeable free verse poems on similar subjects, in similar voices, a landscape of brief epiphanies inflected only here and there by any kind of innovation or intensity.

More significantly, I had just finished writing my first novel (*The Autobiography of My Mother* [1976],) which was a long argument, very wordy, gray on the page, between a lawyer mother whose grammar was convoluted and Germanic, and her flip, talky, hippie daughter. After all those words, all I wanted was to clear a silent space in my head. That was when, not by coincidence, I decided to begin a book I'd been vaguely thinking about for a while. Before I even considered subject or form, though, I saw it spatially: tiny little poems gathered in the center of white space, like a nest of footprints in snow. I saw emptiness first; the words were, in some way, the least of it. Then, when I asked myself what would actually constitute the print on the page, it seemed time to consider the creation of Cora, a New Hampshire woman born and bred, who speaks of her life, her marriage and family, her parents, her town, her growing awareness of what she needs and must demand for herself as a person and as a wife. New Englanders are famously laconic: they use not one more word than they have to, and keep their mouths shut pretty tight when they *are* induced to talk. If Cora were to speak about all those things, each poem would have to—somehow plausibly—break through a kind of silence, the emptiness of that white space so reflective of her own reticence, to be heard.

And that's how I decided that syllabics would give me the control I needed: every syllable would literally be dear; no word would come cheap, no line would brook a single adjective or adverb too many. I remembered that my first encounter with syllabics came way back when I was a college freshman discovering haiku, a form so little known to the world of publishing and of high school writing teachers in 1957 that I'd had to root out dusty old books about it in the Columbia University library basement. It is a little remembered fact that genuine haiku, in the hands of the Japanese, not only deploy their seventeen syllables with care, they also build into themselves, cleverly covert, a hint of the season and even a directionality: the action works horizontally, vertically or diagonally, so that its small narrative has a visual component as well. Directionality did not become a factor in *Cora Fry*, but the idea seemed inescapable that the book, if not every individual poem, should use the round of the year as a significant dramatic and organizing factor—again, I was taking my cue from the most conspicuous facts of New England life in which weather plays as significant a role as love or politics.

As for the syllabics themselves: They gave me that

element of constraint I mentioned, a tight cinch against excess. Among their virtues are invisibility, hence a kind of modesty that could reflect the character of the speaker—they did not encourage a grandiloquence that would have been unlikely for my narrator. They allowed me (the author, not the "I" of the character) the pleasure of playing that game in which two lines can lie beside each other looking utterly unalike, but in fact bearing an identical syllable count; there's an element of sheer delight at knowing you're in control of a factor that few suspect is there. Syllabics not only encourage the visual manipulation of the poem that does show its stuff—("Slipping / between the cool sheets of the / water")—but each little machine (4,4,4,4, or 5,7,5 or similar alternations) functions in a slightly different way to mime the dramatic situation. (In the poem that begins "Storm high," a syllable is added to each successive line until, at the end, after an 11-syllable line, "the wind / snaps off my head" in 4). Altogether, a whole book set in a variety of syllabic configurations gave me the kind of control I feel, say, driving a car with a manual transmission: there's an extra element of responsiveness, hand-made for each situation, for every kind of road condition!

FIVE POEMS FROM *CORA FRY*

•

I want to understand light years.
I live in Oxford, New Hampshire.
When, then, will the light get to me?

•

Fry says a word
in my poor ear
I could do with-
out. In the dark
all of me frowns.
He'll be sorry
when he gets there.

•

I have a neighbor
who is always deep
in a book or two.

High tides of clutter
rise in her kitchen.

Which last longer, words,
words in her bent head,
or the clean spaces

between one perfect
dusting and the next?

•

This is no baby skin—
Chip?
You are a new apple.
If
I take a healthy bite
I
get to the star of seeds,
right?

•

Storm high.
Power's off.

Out on the road
a candle wanders
into the dark night's mouth.

When you begin to see them
there are more dark corners than light.

I could hide in one and not be missed
until the children wake. God protect me.

I am my neighbor's candle wavering down
the long hill, flaring, till the wind
   snaps off my head.

DEBRA BRUCE
ULTRASOUND

While I was a student at the Iowa Writers' Work-
shop in the late 1970's, one of my teachers gave what
me and my classmates thought was a strange assign-
ment: he asked us to write a sonnet. Why would he
do such a thing? we wondered. Rhyme and meter, in
American poetry at least, had been dead for two de-
cades. The sonnet seemed a quaint and artificial form,
and we assumed that our teacher, a well-established
poet who wrote in free verse, was simply reminding
us that it was our duty to know how to construct a
sonnet. My sonnet was dutiful and dull, but I didn't
care. I wrote it in the same spirit in which I might
have tried on my grandmother's corset in a stuffy at-
tic. Thank God poets weren't expected to write these
things anymore.

Several years after I'd left Iowa, I happened to be
reading some poems by Donald Justice, one of the few
contemporary poets who had continued to work in tradi-
tional forms, including the sonnet. My response to his
formal work took me by surprise. His sonnets spoke
to me as intimately and powerfully as any poem in
free verse ever had. Reading Justice's sonnets in 1982
made me want to write a sonnet, a real sonnet, not
just an exercise. I liked the explosive tension of the
form, and the sounds of rhyme and meter moved me
strongly in a way that seemed at once profoundly physical
and psychic. I started experimenting with rhyme and
meter, and I loved it. I had no idea that other poets in
my generation were doing what I was doing, and I

certainly had no idea that there was, according to some, a movement afoot, a return to traditional poetic forms.

Its critics charge that formal poetry is elitist, that it strives to preserve an old social order, one based on obvious injustice and exclusion, that it refuses to ask the troubling and important questions of our time. Formal poetry is charged, by implication, with being racist and sexist. Some feminist poets have argued that a form like the sonnet is essentially intellectual and masculine and could never contain the emotional/animal experience of childbirth. Beneath these charges is, I think, a fundamental confusion about the term "formal poetry." All poetry is formal in the sense that is has form, but formal poetry refers to poetry written in rhyme and meter. And that's all. To write formal poetry, a poet is not required to write about a certain subject, to use certain kinds of diction, or to adopt a certain attitude. Returning to rhyme and meter in the 1990's is not returning to the attitudes and values associated with the formal poems of the 1950's. Many of the poets who are now returning to formal poetry are bringing with them the spirit of the 1960's and 1970's.

Detractors of formal poetry also dismiss it as artificial, but all art is artificial. Defenders of formal poetry, like John F. Nims, often argue that the forms of poetry echo forms in nature, that the iambic beat— u / u / —corresponds to the human heartbeat, and so on. It's clear that rhyme and meter are artificial, but I think that they do echo the primitive repetition and rhythm of human life. At their best, they appeal to our deepest selves.

Last summer I wanted to write a poem about two couples having dinner together—one couple having had a baby after waiting for a long time, the other couple still waiting and hoping to conceive. The poem began in my head with the sound of u / u / u / u / or iambic tetrameter. This meter felt absolutely right for this poem; it came to me before the words did. At the risk of suggesting an analogy that seems outlandish, I want to suggest that in this poem, the meter is functioning like the instrument used by a fertility doctor to take an ultrasound picture of a woman's reproductive system. The machinery is artificial and technological, but what it reveals is a primitive fact—a woman's womb. And the reason this technology exists at all is in response to what is perhaps the most primitive fact of human life—the longing to reproduce ourselves.

Poetic form is artificial, too, but I think at its best it uses rhyme and meter to plumb the most primitive depths of human life.

TWO COUPLES

The mother throws her voice in loops,
up high, above the baby's head,
now brings it down, it swoops and swoops;
she scoops him up and off to bed,
now comes back, flushed, famished, sits,
now bites into the buttered pulp
of an artichoke, a heap of sweets
circling while she and her husband talk
about how the baby's changed their days,
how long they waited. They understand
the other woman who waits and waits.
Last week she had her ovaries scanned.
Who knows what next? The baby's voice—
The father jumps for the bottle.

The other couple, nibbling moist,
glazed bits of apple-babka,
fix their coffee, watching them—
father humming while baby drinks.
She dumps a storm of sugar in,
stirring slowly, trying to think

that life is full, baby or not.
But summer's going, cicadas beat
their crazy song, their timbals taut.
Apples fatten in heat, in heat.
She knows they do. They deepen, drop,
sap-side smack, release their spice.
The nipple slips, the bottle plops
and rolls away, the baby cries.
He's stretched high on his father's thighs,
now dumples down again, now lies,
head hung back on his mother's knees;
looking around and around, he sees
the other couple upside-down.

SONNET 2
(from "The Light They Make")

Deep in her seventh month, my sister dozes
afternoons, her voice still dusky on the phone
a thousand miles away. Distance sizzles
in my ear. I want to hear and I don't
want to—about the afghan she's been weaving,
her legs propped up, how new life crowds her heart,
hurts, takes her breath away, even
the crazy cravings all come true. As far
from her as I've ever been, I wait with her
and I wait alone each month. Buds squeeze,
open, batches of birds hatch, this year

as always, regardless, their first notes tweezed
out high in the trees. Wisteria bulges—boom—
it blooms. My sister's son is born in June.

SONNET 4
(from "The Light They Make")

Wet streets, black trees, a gold leaf smacked
against our bedroom window as I smolder
beside him under a quilt made block by block
by hand by mother's mother, getting older
than she'd told us, bending closer to stitch,
to tug threads tight, then tighter, worrying
she might not finish in time to watch me unlatch
her cedar chest and find it—hurrying.
Relax, my husband says, my ragged sighs
making both of us laugh. *Either way,*
we'll still be happy, right? The only light's
the bright leaves left in trees against the sky.
Of course. It's not the only thing that matters.
Come one good gust, the light they make will shatter.

JULIA BUDENZ
ADMIRATION AND ALLURE

When I write in strict form I do so out of an admiring love and for the sake of an alluring pleasure: moved by love for form itself, for the poetic form in which I am writing, for the beautiful embodiments of form which I have encountered in reading, and drawn to the pleasure that comes from playing with and working with form in all its actuality and all its possibility.

POETA FUI

Kisses upon the doors! The houses fall.
The city falls. The women fix the doors.
The doors must fall since all the afts and fores
Are known. The poet told us of them all.

He skitters with the women through the hall.
He strolls in sandals the ensanguined floors.
The women fix their kisses and he pores
Over the silences behind the wall

Broken and left behind. He left behind
The women and the kisses. There they are.
They have not burned. The kisses still are burning.

And has he turned? And will he surely find
Our road for us? For us will he unbar
That gate? He leads us up this hill of yearning.

MELISSA CANNON
ESSENTIALS

I write in forms for one reason—because they give me pleasure. I love the music of rhyme and meter and the effects you can only create through the use of strict form. I find that forms lead me to the essentials of my material. I enjoy the challenge of learning how each new form operates, how the dynamic of a particular form sculpts the poem. I like the satisfaction of achieving total freedom within a confined space. And I like using what appears to be conventional packaging for unconventional and radical ends.

THE SISTERS

Hot Anger stirs the soup; Grief moves the dust
that's settled in the house, while, at her back,
she hears that cracking cleaver and the thwack
of choice loin pummeled with a lover's lust.
Anger *will* cook up change because she must
break eggs, dump out the whole damned flour sack,
whip cream to froth: then, hungry to attack,
she'll gobble mousse, paté, and blackened crust.

Grief has no appetite. The cloudy air
sifts through her thinning hand. "Goodbye, goodbye,
we'll never meet again, not anywhere,"
the little motes her rag will bury sigh.
But, oh, dear sister, look how, in her care,
the woodwork glosses like a tear-washed eye.

KELLY CHERRY
A FLASHLIGHT OR MAP

Poetic forms, established or nonce, are like maps of places no one's ever been. They lead the writer into uncharted territory; they show the writer where to go, even though they cannot know the way. This paradox is what keeps poetic form eternally interesting. If the writer knew in advance what she would find on her journey through the poem, she would not bother to make it. But she doesn't know; she never knows; she knows only that the form is there like a flashlight or map and that she will see what the form reveals and go where the form takes her. She knows, too, that the form *will* take her somewhere, *will* show her a place never before seen or seen so clearly.

I began writing in forms after I had found, in my opinion anyway, my own voice. I was sitting in on a class taught by that exemplary gentleman Allen Tate. He was fastidious in his personal habits and fastidious about poetic forms too, a stickler for the rules: no rhyming a plural with a singular; no shifting of stress for the sake of scansion, and on and on. My first poems in form seemed to me to be a regression; I felt I had learned to walk, even run, and now could barely crawl, tripping over my painfully counted metrical feet as I toddled and lurched through sonnets and villanelles.

But of course, within a couple of years I could see that encountering Allen Tate was one of the truly lucky events of my literary life. I was working in forms all during the time when most young writers were not. It was certainly not all that I was doing in my writing, but it was one of the things I was doing—working in forms.

I find now that I like to use strong rhymes. I like monosyllabic rhymes. I like using the ordinary rhymes others may tend to avoid. These rhymes suit me; so, for that matter, do quatrains. I am very fond of quatrains and blank verse. I like simple words or perhaps I should say *accurate* words, which, if not always, often, it seems to me, turn out to be simple words. I like a complexity that grows out of thought and feeling and imagery and is not embossed on language baroquely.

There is too much showmanship around, too much that is not an honest attempt to make that journey into the poem that is also a journey into the self.

But to make that journey—that is a great thing to do, it really is. It is something to live your life for.

HISTORY

It is what, to tell the truth, you sometimes feel
That you have had enough of, though of course
You do not really mean that, since you recall
It well enough to know things could be worse
And probably are going to get that way,
But still want a long and memorable life, which
    means
Having to learn more of it day by day,
The names and dates of all the kings and queens
And those less famous who ruled the territory
Known as your heart and now are gone, by one
Dark route or another, from the plot of your story.
But you write on, and are your own best Gibbon,
    And read on, this monumental subject being
    The decline and fall of almost everything.

THE RAIMENT WE PUT ON

Do you remember? We were in a room
With walls as warm as anybody's breath,
And music wove us on its patterning loom,
The complicated loom of life and death.
Your hands moved over my face like small clouds.
(Rain fell into a river and sank, somewhere.)
I moved among your fingers, brushed by the small
    crowds
Of them, feeling myself known, everywhere,
And in that desperate country so far from here,
I heard you say my name over and over,
Your voice threading its way into my ear.
I will spend my days working to discover
The pattern and its meaning, what you meant,
What has been raveled and what has been rent.

THE BRIDE OF QUIETNESS

My sculptor husband, when he *was* mine, possessed
Electrifying energy, humor,
The vital heat of violent force compressed . . .
Contraries in a controlling frame. Few more

Creative and compelling men could fire
The clay I scarcely dared to call my soul.
Shapeless, lacking properties of higher
Existence, it was perfect for the mold

He cast me in: classic receptacle,
A thing for use but full of elegance,
An ode to Greece, forever practical,
Tellingly patterned with the hunt and dance.

My lines were lies. And yet he seemed to see
Aesthetic validation in my form.

I asked him not to draw away from me.
He said he feared he might commit some harm—

Some accidental, inadvertent hurt—
And shatter in an instant all the love
He'd poured out in the effort to convert
My ordinary mind to a work of

Art. And how he shuddered if I assumed
A new position or a point of view!
As if I were a royal vase entombed
After the ancient style, and the issue

Of my movement could only be a change
In where he stood, relative to his wife.
I had to perdure inanimate and strange
And still, if he would justify his life.

For I was the object of his most profound
Research, the crafty subject of his thesis,
And all I had to do to bring him down
Was let my heart break into all those pieces

It ached to break into in any case.
Upon his graduation, when the guests
Had gone, and night was settling on his face,
Raising my voice above his dreams I confessed

That beauty held no truth for me, nor truth
Beauty, but I was made as much of earth
As I had been, barbaric and uncouth,
Enjoined to rhythm, shiftings, blood and birth,

And void of principle. He said he'd father
No children. I could hardly help knowing
That he'd be wrong to trust me any farther.
By sunrise it was clear he would be going

Soon. Now from time to time I see him here
And there. The shoulders have gone slack, the eyes
Conduct a lesser current and I fear
That when they catch me spying, it's no surprise

To him. He always found poetic justice
Amusing, and he knows I wait my turn.
The artist dies; but what he wrought will last
Forever, when I cradle his cold ashes in this urn.

READING, DREAMING, HIDING

*You asked me what is the good of reading the Gospels in
Greek.*   —Czeslaw Milosz, "Readings"

You were reading. I was dreaming
The color blue. The wind was hiding
In the trees and rain was streaming
Down the window, full of darkness.

Rain was dreaming in the trees. You
Were full of darkness. The wind was streaming
Down the window, the color blue.
I was reading and hiding.

The wind was full of darkness and rain
Was streaming in the trees and down the window.
The color blue was full of darkness, dreaming
In the wind and trees. I was reading you.

THE PINES WITHOUT PEER

The pines without peer
Are taller than air.

They grow in the sky,
Their roots in your eye.

And the tops of the pines wave
From the top of the sky, brave

As banners. And the tops
Of the pines are steps

To the high, wheeling
Stars. And your brain is reeling

And the trees are falling,
And you are falling

In a forest, pulled,
Drawn, blinded and mauled,

And you are the ground
And the wound

And the one wild sound.

SANDRA CISNEROS
SPOKEN FORMS

One of the forms that has been, and continues to be, important for me is nursery rhymes, children's chants— forms you learn orally, like jump-rope songs and clapping songs. I've always been attracted to the spoken word, and that's what starts me on a poem. It always starts with a jingle, and then I fit the poem to it.

"Muddy Kid Comes Home" started with a line of overheard conversation in the principal's office at a school where I was working. Some parent had complained because their kid came home muddy. I wrote it in a note to myself: "Muddy kid comes home." That phrase has a beat, a cadence to it, and I built everything else in the poem around that. The jingle comes first; then everything has to conform to one little line. Sometimes it ends up as the title, or it's somewhere in the poem.

I'm always inadvertently using rhyme. I don't ever try; it comes out naturally. My ear has been tuned. My training is looking at a lot of very traditional poets. I started as a child writing poems in fixed forms because those were the models I had. There were some very bad poems in form in my grade school textbook. I was also really fond of the poems in *Alice in Wonderland*, which was my favorite book. I wrote all my poems in little galloping tetrameter/trimeter quatrains. All the poetry I'd seen had form, so that's what I wrote.

Later, when I started learning about prosody in high school, I was amazed that I had been writing in these forms. The poets I liked were an influence: Gwendolyn

Brooks, Emily Dickinson, and Latin American poets. Carl Sandburg was a big influence; I liked poetry that nobody else read. I read E. A. Robinson. I finally taught myself the traditional forms just to know how to do them. In graduate school when I finally took a course in prosody, I was disappointed; I had taught it to myself already, and there wasn't anything new.

I think everyone should take a course in fixed forms. I insist that my students take a prosody course, or that they teach it to themselves, because that information stays with you for life.

MUDDY KID COMES HOME

And mama complains
Mama whose motto
Is mud must remain
Mama who acts
So uppity up

Says mud can't come in
Says mud must stay put
Mama who thinks that
Mud is uncouth

Cannot remember
Can hardly recall
Mud's what I was
When I wasn't at all

But mud must remain
Or Mama complains
Mama who cannot
Remember her name

THE POET REFLECTS ON HER SOLITARY FATE

She lives alone now.
Has abandoned the brothers,
the rooms of fathers
and many mothers.

They have left her
to her own device.
Her nightmares and pianos.
She owns a lead pipe.

The stray lovers
have gone home.
The house is cold.
There is nothing on t.v.
She must write poems.

CHERYL CLARKE
Thoughts on Form and Formalism
and My Uses of Them...

The longing to be a technician makes me want to write a sonnet or a sestina. But I flee the tenacity required to perfect any form. I do it—the form—to be rebellious and sometimes to be reserved. How can I reflect my black self in the form, how can I speak my contempt from inside the master's formula? To be silly. For irony. To control the language of difficult emotions, as in "Rondeau," a feminist critique of the cult of romance. Form can put pain at some distance. I value a certain tightness that the form can give me, whether I use it loosely or strictly. I've got one or two secret haikus, but have not attained the humility of that spareness.

Most of my formal poems began that way. Some would not be controlled otherwise. Should I try a crown of sonnets for my poem on the civil rights movement? I often don't feel clever enough. I feel too self-conscious, as if an African-American poet should not be using European conventions. Then I remember Gwen Brooks, Robert Hayden, Countee Cullen, Phillis Wheatley. So, the forms, like most things Western—for good or for ill—are my history too.

What goes around comes around, or The proof is in the pudding

*Truthfulness, honor, is not something which springs
ablaze of itself: it has to be created between people...*
　　　　　　　　—Adrienne Rich, "Women and Honor"

A woman in my shower crying.
All I can do is make potato salad
and wish I hadn't been caught lying.

I dust the chicken for frying
pretending my real feelings too much a challenge
to the woman in my shower crying.

I forget to boil the eggs, time is flying,
my feet are tired, my nerves frazzled,
and I wish I hadn't been caught lying.

Secondary relationships are trying.
I'd rather roll dough than be hassled
by women in my shower crying.

Truth is clarifying.
Pity it's not more like butter.
I wish I hadn't been caught lying.

Ain't no point denying,
my soufflé won't even flutter.
I withhold from the woman in my shower crying
afraid of the void I filled with lying.

TORTOISE AND BADGER

I'll still follow you, primordial
thing, out of the swamp to the vague median

and beyond. Your shell is hardly cordial
and my spiky fur has gone seedy
with the strain of another defenseless fight
with you, your sparse hairs under my claws.
Want to tickle the back of your Chelonite
and squeeze your small snout in my paws.

Want to turn you over to your soft belly,
silly, hungry me. You don't have much meat.
Just layers of sad and pleading, scaly
skin. Finally, I'll kiss your dancing feet.

You can scuttle all you want to down the trail.
I'll still scurry right behind and bite your tail.

RONDEAU

They are bodies left unburied.
Instead of roaming the underworld they've tarried
to bring their nomadic anxiety
to my world with little propriety.
I'd rather them waylaid in Staten Island, unferried.

Sit next to this one here, pass her, there's that one
   there.
This one's pretty, that one tall, her there, she's fair.
Haunt my silence, hurt my silence, make me crazy.
They are bodies.

I try to act modern, but still I'm worried.
We sleep together every night but still I'm worried
that she or she loves you more expertly sexually
than me obsessed by her or her like voices of insanity.
Provocative and sexy nonmonogamy in theory.
But they are bodies.

CATHERINE DAVIS
THE AIR WE BREATHED

Poets of my generation did not consider formal po-
etry an anomaly. Rather, it was the air we breathed.
In our younger years many of us were reading Wallace
Stevens, Marianne Moore, Ezra Pound, T.S. Eliot, e.e.
cummings, and Hart Crane, most of whom had writ-
ten both formal verse and free verse. The exception
was William Carlos Williams, who, at least in his known
published work, wrote only free verse. On the other
hand, W.B. Yeats, E.A. Robinson, and Robert Frost wrote
only formal poetry. We were also reading, of course,
the poetry of an earlier generation: Thomas Hardy, Walt
Whitman, and Emily Dickinson. The generation that
most directly influenced many of us, and certainly me,
were, except for John Crowe Ransom, all born in the
twentieth century and were not only our mentors but
also sometimes literally our teachers and advisers. In
those early years the poets who deeply influenced me
were largely formalists; they included, besides Ran-
som, the southern poets Allen Tate and Robert Penn
Warren and, later, Louise Bogan, J.V. Cunningham, and
Yvor Winters. All of these poets of whatever genera-
tion provided me and my contemporaries with the whole
spectrum, from formal to free verse, of possibilities in
writing poetry. It is astonishing to me now how little
prejudice there was then about writing one kind of
poetry over another.

The shift to free verse came, I think, in the early
1960's after the publication in 1959 of Robert Lowell's
Life Studies, a book surprising in many ways from Lowell,

a passionate traditionalist, not least because of the prominence of free verse in it. Then in 1962 William Carlos Williams' book *Pictures from Brueghel* came out. Both books had, I believe, a tremendous influence on the poets of my age. By that time, having finally received my B.A. at the age of thirty-seven, I had come as a graduate student to the Iowa Workshop, and it was an important change for me in every way. I began to write, much to my own surprise, free verse while continuing to write formal poetry; others changed to free verse for good. As the decade went along it was formal poetry that began to seem an anomaly, and it has been pretty much that way ever since. But I could never see why I should not practise both, as so many poets had done in the early twentieth century. Neither one is superior to the other.

BELONGINGS

Nothing about the first abandonment
In which the loose leaves lost their grip and slid
Dumbly, obliquely down to lie for days
On porches, lawns, and walks or skid along
The streets indifferently—nothing about
The way the birds took off, black against white
White skies, or the days slumped and the dismal
   ground
Beneath her faded out—unsettled her.
These were routine.
                It was the backward look
Of certain hours and how the warm air lagged,
The wind wavered and stopped, the leaves hung on;
It was the unexpectedly dense light
Late afternoons like hoarded gold, holding
For her the old effects, the diverse trash

Of other times, belongings held too long
Because they once had served, although they served
No longer, and to which she thus belonged.
Had she not, too long now, resolved that all
Loved grievous things, though they should prove the
    whole,
Would be, once and for all, swept up and out?

So, when a fine, cold, desolating rain
And wind, needling and nudging her, began,
She felt the comfort of their empty hands.
Had she believed that rain cried or that wind
Was querulous, she might have heard in them
A general reluctance to be done.
But as it was, it was the usual drift
Of all expendables, reminding her
What she belonged to, what belonged to her.

THE YEARS

Then came the year of fires.
The burnings always took—
Because of the interminable freeze,
The way the sick elms shook—
The form of lost desires,
The only longing, surcease.

Within the fires there stirred
The years, the years of rage;
Could fire, then, not exhaust
What tears could not assuage?
The flames' tongues all demurred.
And then, to be sure to be lost,

Within myself I knelt
To the venomous flames as they rose
From the dreamless dark and stilled

The years of unrepose
And unrelease; I felt
Tired to the bone and chilled.

What year, which I begin
With the dying sound in my ears
Of the fire's rattle and hiss,
Afraid, because of the years,
Not to be looking in
And looking out, is this?

OUT OF WORK, OUT OF TOUCH, OUT OF SORTS
(Dupont Circle, Washington, D.C.)

Already past mid-June,
And something should be done;
I sit all afternoon
Feeling both out of touch
And out of sorts, and sun
Myself on a bench near
The fountain; there's not much
On a temporary basis
That I know how to do.
What will my coming here,
Summer spent, amount to?
One of my wild-goose chases?

Carved on the fountain's base
Are the bare names and dates
Of the man whom this place,
A wreath of water, leaf,
And stone, commemorates;
Wind, Ocean, Stars as three
Figures in high relief
Circle the shaft. The hand
That undertook his story

For the passersby and me
Lost it in allegory—
The thing is much too grand.

The passersby pass by.
They look instead at me,
Or those they meet, as I
At them. The Admiral
Himself would no doubt be
Surprised, were he to pass
His lost memorial.
The mere water striking
The bowl's edges, the trim
Bushes, young leaves and grass,
Which also might please him,
Are much more to our liking.

All winter long this scene—
The walks, spokes of a wheel,
The civil gray and green
Of everyday concerns,
The Circle like a reel
On which the gigantic thread
Of traffic sings and turns,
The staid fountain's commotion—
Turned in the mind and brought,
For every move that led
Forward, a quicker thought
In steady countermotion.

Images of the past
Simplify as they grow
Centrifugal and vast;
The days all run together;
The long, eccentric snow
Of being somewhere else
Falls through perfect weather;

Starlings once seen flying
In pairs, wing guiding wing,
With the wild irregular pulse
Of love in late-found spring,
Circle together, crying.

Nothing is quite like that—
This city, least of all;
I think of the times I've sat
In the shadow of events
Faceless, impersonal.
What stone colossus' hands
Altered the private sense
Of how much one can master?
That others also grope
Shapes what one understands,
Facing the downward slope
Of a decade's near-disaster.

I almost learned, for once,
To take things as they come;
So now the eye confronts,
Not the past spun beyond
Itself, but the humdrum
Comings and goings of such
As momently respond
Only to what is living,
Momently changed within.
I sense, almost in touch,
But minding what has been,
The present's gift of giving.

RITA DOVE
AN INTACT WORLD

Sonnet literally means "little song." The sonnet is a *heile Welt*, an intact world where everything is in sync, from the stars down to the tiniest mite on a blade of grass. And if the "true" sonnet reflects the music of the spheres, it then follows that any variation from the strictly Petrarchan or Shakespearean form represents a world gone awry.

Or does it? Can't form also be a talisman against disintegration? The sonnet defends itself against the vicissitudes of fortune by its charmed structure, its beautiful bubble. All the while, though, chaos is lurking outside the gate.

The ancient story of Demeter and Persephone is a modern dilemma as well: there is a point where the mother can no longer protect her children, and both mother and child must come to terms with this. In her grief, Demeter defies the law of nature by neglecting her agricultural duties so that the crops die. In varying degrees she is admonished or pitied by the other gods for the depth of her grief. She refuses to accept her fate, she strikes out against the Law; and it is this neglect that triggers Olympus to reach compromise with Hades. Demeter may still defy natural law when she grieves every Fall and Winter; but she must act "normal" for the rest of the year.

Sonnets seemed the proper mode for this work-in-progress—and not only in homage and as counterpoint to Rilke's *Sonnets to Orpheus*. Much has been said about the many ways to "violate" the sonnet in the service

of American speech or modern love or whatever; I will
simply say that I like how the sonnet comforts even
while its prim borders (but what a pretty fence!) are
stultifying; one is constantly bumping up against the
Law. The Demeter/Persephone cycle of betrayal/re-
generation seems ideally suited for this form, since all
three—mother-goddess, daughter, and poet—are strug-
gling to sing in their chains.

PERSEPHONE UNDERGROUND

If I could just touch your ankle, he whispers, *there
on the inside, above the bone*—leans closer,
breath of lime and peppers—*I know I could
make love to you.* She considers
this, secretly thrilled, though she wasn't quite
sure what he meant. He was good
with words, words that went straight to the liver.
Was she falling for him out of sheer boredom—
cooped up in this anything-but-humble dive, stone
gargoyles leering and brocade drapes licked with
    fire?
Her ankle burns where he described it. She sighs
just as her mother aboveground stumbles, is caught
by the fetlock—bereft in an instant—
while the Great Man drives home his desire.

HISTORY

Everything's a metaphor, some wise
guy said, and his woman nodded, wisely.
Why was this such a discovery
to him? Why did history
happen only on the outside?

She'd watched an embryo track an arc
across her swollen belly from the inside
and knew she'd best
think *knee*, not *tumor* or *burrowing mole*, lest
it emerge a monster. Each craving marks
the soul: splashed white upon a temple the dish
of ice cream, coveted, broken in a wink,
or the pickle duplicated just behind the ear. *Every wish
will find its symbol*, the woman thinks.

POLITICAL
(for Breyten Breytenbach)

There was a man spent seven years in hell's circles—
no moon or starlight, shadows singing
their way to slaughter. We give him honorary status.
There's a way to study freedom but few have found
it; you must talk yourself to death and then beyond.
Even Demeter keeps digging
towards that darkest miracle,
the hope of finding her child unmolested.

This man did something ill-advised, for good reason.
(I mean he went about it wrong.)
And paid in shit, the world is shit and shit
can make us grown. It is becoming the season
she was taken from us. Our wail starts up
of its own accord, is mistaken for song.

"BLOWN APART BY LOSS..."

Blown apart by loss, she let herself go—
wandered the neighborhood hatless, breasts
swinging under a ratty sweater, crusted

mascara blackening her gaze. It was a shame,
the wives whispered, to carry on so.
To them, wearing foam curlers arraigned
like piglets to market was almost debonair,
but an uncombed head?—not to be trusted.

The men watched more closely, tantalized
by so much indifference. Winter came early and still
she frequented the path by the river until
one with murmurous eyes pulled her down to size.
Sniffed Mrs. Franklin, ruling matron, to the rest:
Serves her right, the old mare.

SUZANNE J. DOYLE
WHEN THE BALLERINA DOESN'T POINT HER TOES

The other night I attended a performance of the San Francisco Ballet and saw a new dance choreographed by Val Caniparoli. It was a light-hearted piece about love that involved lots of pairing and unpairing of partners, and it actually got some laughs, which is rare at the ballet. As soon as the male lead lifted the ballerina from the floor her toes sprang up at right angles to her legs. Not surprisingly, when the ballerina doesn't point her toes on stage she looks funny. Why? Because it defies our formal expectations and thereby creates a tension which, in this case, we dispel by laughing. And those ballerina's toes just happen to illustrate what I consider one of the greatest advantages of working in poetic form: you have a norm, artificial as it may be, from which to deviate for dramatic effect. I love to deviate.

But not so often as to lose the definition of the metric line. Even free verse can't escape the underlying rhythm of the English language, alternating unstressed-stressed syllables called iambs—which also happen to echo the beat of the heart. It is a rhythm I never tire of hearing, reassuring in its predictability, yet as infinitely capable of variation as the human voices it informs: "the barge she sat in like a burnished throne"; "I'll have a beer, a burger, and some fries." And while, of course, there is nothing inherently better about poems written in formal measures, it seems foolish to me for a poet to ignore the proven power of this rhythmical pattern in the language. Like ballet dancing without toe shoes, it can be done, and done beautifully, but there are some heights you just can't reach, some lines you just can't realize without the shoes. I love those heights; I love those lines.

THIS SHADE

This is my mother's childhood home, my own.
Late summer: bushels warp in orchard grass.
The apples drop into an insect drone
Pervasive as this shade; we sense the past.

Mnemonic as the taste of late, warm fruit,
This arbor and its sentimental blur
Of earth and roses resurrect those brute,
Voracious children we forget we were.

The broad leaves stir along the vine—intrusion
Gentle as this present—where my mother
Steps beneath a vegetable confusion
Savage as our hold on one another.

Beyond this tangle of espaliers, noon
Passes in the shadow of a perfect arc;
Here bees have sucked the ripe grapes dry, and soon
The skins will settle, sweeter for the dark.

SOME GIRLS
(for Andrea Vargas)

The risk is moral death each time we act,
And every act is whittled by the blade
Of history, pared down to brutal fact,
The fact: we only want what we degrade.

No beauty in the glass makes our loss good,
No hero in the wings can take the stage,
The clash of blood at war with its own blood
Intoxicates us with colossal rage.
A cold beer and the young moon's tender horns
Are shining on the table where we spar
Like women gladiators, bred and born
To wear our father's breastplates, greaves and scars.
There's something not quite right here. We can't talk
Like some girls, who'd say, "Hell, the bastards broke
    our hearts."
We are a different kind of tough; we hawk
Our epic violence in bleak bars, in bed, in art.

HELL TO PAY

When the children are asleep and our old bed
Fills with the drama of your dreams, I head
Downstairs to double check the locks and pour
Neat bourbon down, just like I did before
I ever locked a door, back when I blazed by night
Through danger in a yellow whiskey light.
I am again the wildhearted and lonely,
To whom the angel will appear, the only
Angel I have known, who drags her wings
On dance hall floors while some bright jukebox sings
Of sadness gone too sweet, and I am caught
Up in the arms of all the feeling I have fought.
Against that torn mouth no kiss comes to bless,
I answer to the shame I can't confess,
The old wound coiled up bitterly in me,
The one your love relieves but cannot free.
Hers is the power of darkness, fierce, defiled,
To which fate led me willing as a child,
And though I kneel to love to serve each day,
I know in time there will be hell to pay.

RHINA P. ESPAILLAT
WHY I LIKE TO DANCE IN A BOX

First, it's fun, as all play is fun; the arts, after all, are a form of play. Formal verse feels good to the ear, to the whole body, like handclapping and foot-tapping. It satisfies something in me that wants to dance, that has never outgrown play.

Second, it's play organically related to the nature of poetry, to the impulse that underlies writing. It says that reality is what it is, and I may not be able to change it or do justice to it or even endure it, but I can make something out of my perception of it, something that wasn't here before. The box is a given, but I do have the option of dancing in it.

Third, it's an act of faith, a conviction based on no evidence at all that behind the huge disorder surrounding the little bits of artificial order we create for ourselves there is some real order—or better still, harmony—even if we can't see it or hear it. I dance in a box to tell the harmony that I want to move with it, submit to it, if it will have me.

And finally, it feels natural. I feel at home in the apparent constraints of formal verse, as I've never felt at home in the apparent freedom of free verse. Formal verse more accurately parallels the way I live, working inside the rules but straining away from them, getting away with as much disruption as I can without actually destroying the pattern, thumbing my nose while looking respectful, actually *being* respectful of the idea of order while seeming to thumb my nose.

METRICS

I like the clattering of hoof on street
Signalling "horse"; slow course of fruit
From earth, air, water, sun and root
Through branch to ripened flower makes it sweet;

Under soul's music, the eternal tone,
I like mortality to play the bass;
Love and the dancer's gestures must be grace
Wrested from bone.

All things, however magneted by cause,
Should bear their nature's imprint to the end;
Should shadow forth the whole to which they tend,
But keep small laws.

JULIE FAY
A KIND OF SURVIVAL

I find that structure is more compelling than it is restricting. As a good plot keeps you turning the pages in a novel, rhyme or repetition asks you to keep writing. One of the poems included here—"Dear Marilyn"— was like that for me. It's one from a series of epistolary poems Marilyn Hacker and I sent to one another over about a year's time—a correspondence we still occasionally tune into. (Marilyn's poems were published in her collection *Love, Death and the Changing of Seasons*.) We were both going through rather tumultuous personal relationships at the time, she in New York, and I in Vence, France. I'd get a poem from her, and have to answer it in kind. I found some relief in transforming very painful events into sardonic nursery-rhyme-like letters to Marilyn. One week there'd be a happy ending, the next a tragic one. It was a very emotionally charged time and the overflow came out as poems. Though not as austere or subtle as poems like Bishop's insistent "One Art," my poems came out of that kind of necessity to move through pain by writing about it and thereby imposing some order on the emotional chaos. Some of those poems were a kind of survival.

Later, I assigned myself the task of writing a round of Sicilian forms that dealt with a trip my husband and I took from Nice to Sicily. That's what "Words" came out of, a form invented to capture the fast rhythms of new love and new places.

DEAR MARILYN

Dear Marilyn:

Think of this as chapter two, a second
installment, if you will. I'm on the hill
calling down the muse, reckoning
for amusement how many men I have or will

have had since I left home. I'm tired.
My body's bruised. I keep losing track
of things. What pills and when have I
taken and how many? I needed to black

the other night out, so it was at least seven
valium... I'd been writhing on the bed (alone)
wondering, screaming, how to even
out the score. (But what's the game?) Not home,

L. had left her sleep-pills out, barbs inviting
as smooth-faced pebbles on the bed
of a long, warm river. Crying
at my lack of guts, I said

if I can just get through one more night
the next day might be better. The message
of this chapter is to keep passing by
the chance, to keep passing windows

left open (it's been said before). So I counted out
how many pills to take, enough
to get me through the night blacked out
but able in the morning to get up.

It's embarrassing to admit to these
nightly adventures of self-abuse. I hate
people who wallow in this kind of me me me
self-pity, tune it like an eight

cylinder engine. I mean,
who cares? Next day I woke up and went
to town, sat down, read what I'd been
writing to you the day before, lent

my lighter to the town's male whore
and began another day and night
of getting even. Of course
the guy wears black, the stereotyped

villain from a grade-C western.
I picked out Vence's worst
to pick me up, went up to what he termed
the best view in town to get what I deserved.

When this old-man primadonna pulled a knife
on me in bed I told him he should keep
his brand of kinky to himself, and while
he was in the kitchen, hid it neatly

under cowboy boots in his armoire.
He came back to bed, armed
with a new supply of champagne and caviar.
He thinks I'm charming.

He wants to buy me one of Lillian's creations.
I can't stand to see him
and can't avoid him. All the relations
I've had gather in the bar at six.

I might stop soon, might not. Can't write,
can't stop. Can't eat, can't sleep.
So when the other night
a young, fair-faced redhead seemed

tender, rubbing my tired feet, gave me
a massage, I made him sleep here.

He *is* tender. He's a fag, it seems,
sometimes, others not. There

are, when I count them, so far
this season six men I've come to terms with,
six men I've made bizarre,
hateful love with. No, it's

not quite true. Two of them
I wanted in a better way. Two
of them I've hurt, and when
this installment gets to you

number seven will have been and gone.
Last night, he was here for dinner.
French. Polite. He's all wrong
for this game of take nothing, winner.

WORDS

We are taking the boat to Sicily.
We are bound to each other visibly.
We hurdle a blue chain cautiously

on the bow of the boat bound for Sicily.
We drink wine and make love noisily.
On the deck as the waves beat choppily,

our cries spray where Sirens frantically
sang alarms to the boats bound for Sicily.
Our lives and the night stream by dizzily.

While we two are a ship bound for Sicily
carting gold, stolen goods and mystery,
cresting waves, cresting pleasure, sizzling.

ANNIE FINCH
ILLICIT COMMUNION

If I know the form of a poem in advance, I'm less likely to know how the poem will turn out than if it were in free verse. Meter led me into—and out of—my own labyrinths when I could no longer "think of anything to say" in free verse. I was raised to feel that form was illicit, and experiments in form still feel for me like forays into the outlawed wilderness. Because of the excitement this generates, and because of the absorbing challenges of formal poetic craft, communion with form can distract me, so that the poem comes out by itself.

Language is the medium where I feel the human past and future as most palpably present, in the roots and tips of the words that are always invisibly working their way through us all. Right now, poetic form heightens this sense of language for me in two ways: first, it helps me listen more acutely for language's physical and aesthetic as well as representative powers. Second, forms, like words, have an evolving history of their own that amazes me, opening doors into the rhythms of other minds.

DICKINSON

Of all the lives I cannot live,
I have elected one

to haunt me till the margins give
and I am left alone.

One life will vanish from my voice
and make me like a stone—

one that the falling leaves can sink
not over, but upon.

FOR GRIZZEL MCNAUGHT (1709-1792)

Bound in the women who chain by,
sometimes I reach out with alarm,
stopped sometimes by an old reply.

The chain connects me to the farm
that was your ground and fed your sheep.
The last thing you might wish is harm,

but the trees are frantic if I sleep.
The gold that springs out from your tomb
is bitter. And I want to keep

the branches that burst from your broom,
the anger of the fertile tears
you knew in your low-ceilinged room.

A REPLY FROM HIS COY MISTRESS

Sir, I am not a bird of prey:
A Lady does not seize the day.
I trust that brief Time will unfold
our youth, before he makes us old.
How could we two write lines of rhyme
were we not fond of numbered Time
and grateful to the vast and sweet
trials his days will make us meet?

The Grave's not just the body's curse;
no skeleton can make a verse!
So while this numbered World we see,
let's sweeten Time with poetry,
and Time, in turn, may sweeten Love
and give us time our love to prove.
You've praised my eyes, forehead, breast;
you've all our lives to praise the rest.

SAPPHICS FOR PATIENCE

But there—something rests on your hand and even
lingers, though the wind all around is asking
it to leave you. Passing the windy passage,
you have been chosen.

Seed. Like dust or thistle it sits so lightly
that your hand while holding the trust of silk gets
gentle. Seed like hope has come, making stillness.
Wish in the quiet.

If I stood there—stopped by a windy passage—
staring at my hand—which is always open—
hopeful, maybe, not to compel you, I'd wish
something like patience.

JOAN AUSTIN GEIER
ON WRITING FORMAL POETRY

For me, formal composition involves an extra challenge. Can I take a rigid vessel (usually a form originated centuries ago) and fill it with living, fluid poetry? Like the ongoing relationship between water and its retainers, the experience can be peaceful or exhilarating, powerful, sometimes fearful. I am much indebted to poet Alfred Dorn for an understanding of modern and traditional poetics, and for inspiration in adapting contemporary techniques to metrical/formal poetry.

ON YOUR TWENTY-FIRST BIRTHDAY

My son, you are a sweet bitter shadow
among the fuschia blossoms of sibling
roots and vines; a silent tornado
in my breast; the bottled genie scribbling
this line—but I will not have you crippling
my breath, nor will I sit with vacant stare
fingering pain. I will rise from this chair

and prepare an ordinary meal.
I wonder what it would have been. Might there be
a special pasta on the table? I feel
an odd disconnection with what I see—
your smiling father, brothers, sister. We
joke and pass the platters. It's the same
throughout the meal. I do not say your name

as if you matter less than the ragout.
But I don't forget the blue-born flower
I never saw. Darling, I remember you,
your frightened squirming as I gnawed each hour,
worried, tense. Was I your destroyer?
Had I sent joy, you'd have waited, surely,
not come with diseased lungs, prematurely,

a cord-strangled, prenatal suicide.
Green phantoms forced a cup upon my nose
and as I flailed and sank I cried,
"Save my baby." Gassed blind, I prayed and rose
to surgical light. Need for you unfroze me,
left me screaming, clutching, crying.
The nurse said you were blue and likely dying.

You fought three hours; then your father came
to my clean, white bed above the river.
I told him I'd given you his name.
His eyes glistened, spilled. My son, your father's
tears are rare. I bless them, my lover's
gift, the sweet kernel that lies beneath the husk.
I knew he loved us both. That was enough

to strengthen me through the visitors.
The doctor, weary, not a bit like God,
asked permission to look inside you. Tears
choked, twisted my tongue. I could only nod
you over to the knife, taking that odd
chance that someday life would redeem
your death. The knife, the wound, the scream

inside. I turned away, unencumbered
by you. No need now to tuck a pillow
beneath a fruitful belly. You are remembered
in cans and can'ts. I can turn. I can't will you
back. I can smile again, but, little fellow,

I can't find you though I can spryly caper
like a neurotic chimp around the paper

springing rhythms, slanting rhymes among the facts.
Where are you now, small flesh of my flesh?
"We will bury him in a small, white box,"
the Grey Lady said, "wrapped in a white plush
blanket." Out loud, I made a wish
to have one glimpse before you were entombed.
She blinked, didn't answer. Were you rewombed

already (and she too kind to tell me),
a bottled curio, displayed in formaldehyde
in some lab? I know I always will be
derelict, the need to know you unsatisfied.
Each time I tried to ask again I cried.
The simple, necessary words never came
and I drew my sheets around me like shame.

This evening an almost familiar face slips
among the candles, a teasing young man
tall as your brothers; around his lips
a twinkle, a taste for strawberry jam.
I know you when you come, I sense your name.
But last night, in the corner of a room
that once was mine, I watched the red moon climb

over an empty, yellow bassinet
and heard a phantom baby's plaintive wail.
My breasts ached to feed it. In the dim light
your father's naked shoulders seemed not real.
I touched his back softly, softly and kept still.

Somewhere bottled up, right now, a hunger twists
under sealed eyelids. There is anger in your small fists,
and between us scorched distances of wishes.
I blow the candles and rise to clear the dishes.

SARAH GORHAM
A DANCING FLOOR

The poems included here are part of a sonnet sequence tracing the rise and fall of the last Empress of China. Tz'u-Hsi entered the Imperial Palace as a fifth-place concubine. When she birthed a son, she rose quickly through the ranks to become empress at the age of twenty-six. Her last act was to appoint a two-year-old to her throne, and the Imperial System collapsed shortly after in 1912.

But, why sonnets?

Because one theme of the series is *duality*: heart and mind, ambition and passivity, nurture and destruction. I imagined a woman forced to balance in herself many opposing forces.

The use of form parallels and enhances this duality, for the formalist too engages conflicting impulses. In writing a sonnet, for example, I am caught between the natural cadences of speech (which sometimes must break the traditional metrical convention of iambic pentameter) and the strict rhyming pattern.

It is a potent rivalry. The discipline required frustrates me. It also forces me to reach like the Empress, to extend my vocabulary beyond the easy image or overused statement. As the American Buddhist Pema Chodron said: "The obstacle is a great teacher."

The sonnet is a willful creature. And my engagement with it must appear effortless, pleasing to the ear. Music accompanies every major event in the Empress's life, beginning with the march-like tones of "Instructions from a Chinese Love Manual." The narrative pull of the series is towards harmony, the resolution of opposites.

I came late to the use of form, and although I still
write at least half my work in open verse, I find the
puzzle of a sonnet, villanelle, or acrostic satisfies a need
for both daring and order. Like laying a good parquet
floor, a dancing floor.

THE WHITE TIGER LEAPS
(from "Notes From a Chinese Love Manual")

He jumps from behind, flying like a shard
of glass or maybe cloud. The terror lies
in not knowing which. Too proud
to turn around, you memorize
the light before you, jade, flowers.
You think: I see this, I can
control something. Naked, on all fours,
you bury the desire to run,
imagine instead, his adoring yellow eyes
and claws closed up. And when
he takes you by surprise
you hang on to your vision
of roses and jewels and falling
light. Quickly he devours it all.

PRINCESS PARADE

Tea for the Emperor arrives on a tray
barely tasted, unspoiled.
So do the ladies
who ride high above the soil
through the Gate of Humble Birth
to the Hall of Purity. A wing,
the poet said, is neither heaven nor earth
and the ladies comb their hair like wings

or cresting waves, eager to set down
in one place or another. They clutch
good-luck boxes of baby shoes, brown
butterflies. The Emperor says this much:
I like the one with Sorrow Brows,
her face a frieze of falling snow.

THE EMPRESS RECEIVES THE HEAD OF A TAIPING REBEL

This is the right gift for a poet
who enjoys ordering the sound of water,
who rises late and draws tight
blinds against the advancing sun. She uncovers
the wooden box, her mouth for one second
gaping, resembling his. Oh, how much his expression
contains! The abandon, the sureness, the moment
he stumbled and the sword spread his throat
wide open. To have it all here,
written down! Frozen possibility, like a fruit
that ripens only once in a thousand years.
She caught him in the act of ripening, and tonight,
like a fruit, he'll hang on a tree,
whispering to her of longevity.

JANE GREER
ART IS MADE

Since 1981 the magazine I edit and publish, *Plains Poetry Journal*, has had as a guiding motto: "No subject is taboo, but poetry is art, and art is made." A good poem is like a good British murder mystery. Its metrical or rhyme form gives the reader hints of what word or sound or rhythm is coming next. Then the poet's job is simultaneously to satisfy and surprise the reader. Rhymes that are carefully "off" (what I like to think of as "itchingly close") and meters that contain carefully placed irregularities are more interesting to write than predictably formed poems, because I must choose from a much wider selection of rhyming words. A poet who doesn't pay attention to metrics (of which rhyme is just one species) has an entire universe of words to choose from and refuses to choose. I limit myself to a (still rather wild) palette of words and stress patterns and dally over the pleasure of the choosing itself, with the hope, all the time, that what I choose will give my reader goose bumps the way it does me.

That's the oldest and really, to me, the only point of poetry: delight, in as many forms as possible. To refuse rhyme or meter is to limit the delight. And no one has poetic license to do that.

RODIN'S "GATES OF HELL"

This is too tall, dark wave of soul
tossed molten up against the wall,
blown out from some vile secret hole,

sinners spit from the bilge of Hell,
half-melted in fire where time has frozen.
Starved for the firm flesh of his child,
Ugolino in highest treason
breaks his fast but is never filled,
love eating love, time out of time.
Back-to-back, bronze unrelenting
lovers suffer, their once-sublime
bodies grown muscle-bound with wanting.
Paolo and Francesca fall
eternally though they cling and clamber,
lust and unfaithfulness a pall,
passion their torture to remember.
Torsos and arms I somehow know
are thrust, broken, from the black gulf;
heads of the damned emerge from shadow,
ghosts of all sorrow, of myself.
Shades in each other's shadows quicken;
by their sad breath the bronze is tarnished.
Still, great unpeopled breakers beckon.
This is too large. And too unfinished.

EMILY GROSHOLZ
ART AND SCIENCE

In the decade after I turned sixteen, I covered a couple of meters of paper with poetic five finger exercises. (The proof is in three or four cartons stashed out of sight in my office.) Without any reliable topics or firm experience, I nonetheless dimly felt that I was working on the "music" of my poems, and that establishing a musical line was somehow essential to my project. When I was in my late twenties, my friend Catherine Iino made two invaluable remarks about my writing in the midst of a poetry group discussion. She observed that it wasn't really necessary to capitalize the beginning of every line of a poem; and that I usually wrote blank verse. I was quite surprised to discover that what my ear had been unconsciously listening for all those years, and what my hand had finally learned how to produce, was iambic pentameter. But there it was, reams of it.

In her review of my first book, *The River Painter* (University of Illinois, 1984), Mary Kinzie also noticed this feature, or peculiarity, of my writing; she further pointed out its inherent weakness (formal monotony) and made me for the first time conscious of a device that I had been using to relieve the monotony, the interspersing of trimeter lines. Her remarks are, as always, worth quoting:

> Emily Grosholz is effortless in the iambic mode.
> Even in seemingly unmetrical, or at least unsymmetrical
> lines, the processional gait of blank verse is the audible

norm.... She sprinkles trimeter lines among the pen-
tameters, a technique that detains—holds back—the
magniloquent blank-verse effect. These reduced lines
also permit her to catch her breath, focus on the tru-
est syllable expression, which may be briefer than
the decasyllabic line, before launching out again in
iambic pentameter, fully armed to wrest large expe-
rience from the even larger and more forbidding blank-
verse tradition. Staying actions like the reduced trimeter
line are doubly helpful for poets like Grosholz, who
can do the pentameter in their sleep and hence fall
too easily back into heavily stichic passages where
the lines are end-stopped, unvaried by caesuras, and
metrically regular, varying only in the use of pyr-
rhics (unstressed feet). (*American Poetry Review*, March/
April 1984: 42).

Once I'd read this articulation of my own practice, I
started to count feet as I wrote, trying to use the trimeter
lines with greater care in the context of blank verse,
and by and large suppressing the tetrameter lines I'd
let in before because I wasn't really keeping track. Many
of what I think are the most successful poems in my
latest book, *Eden* (Johns Hopkins University Press, 1992),
are written in this metrical mode that I, stricken by
the computer age, can't help calling my default mode.
And the reason is that these poems were written in
the face of imperious experience: I had to get them
down, and get them down fast in the interstices of my
overstuffed life. So I used the formal devices I knew
would work for me.

All the same, I have from time to time played with
other formal devices, and hope in the future to em-
ploy them at leisure, if I ever have any again. I've tried
writing short line verse, which is usually not so much

dimeter or trimeter in some particular foot, but rather accentual verse with two or three beats. And, in my opinion, my accentual verse so far is a bit shaky. I've also made attempts at rhyming schemes, most notably in my sonnets. But the rhyme is almost always slant and I have never perfectly honored the scheme; indeed, often I was never quite sure which one I'd picked. Congruity of sound is an important dimension of the music of my poems, but it is more likely to be managed by assonance and consonance, slant-rhyme, and internal rhyme than by full end rhyme. In this I am a child of my half-century.

Lately I've noticed two tendencies in my writing, which strain away from iambic pentameter. On the one hand, I've been saying famous tetrameter poems over and over to myself ("Loveliest of trees, the cherry now," "Whose woods these are, I think I know," "Oh God, our help in ages past") in an attempt to secure that slightly shorter line-length, which lends itself to poems of special elegance and concision. On the other hand, I've been tending more and more to begin all or most lines with a stressed syllable: this could be just a truncated iamb, with the light first syllable left off, or pushed back up to the preceding line. Or it could be the first step in exploring the possibilities of trochaic feet. Who knows, perhaps after awhile I'll move on to dactyls. In any case, the art and science of metrics has proved itself a source of illumination, occasional tears, and amusement in my career as a poet, and I look forward to the next stage of discovery.

EDEN

In lurid cartoon colors, the big baby
dinosaur steps backwards under the shadow
of an approaching tyrannosaurus rex.
"His mommy going to fix it," you remark,
serenely anxious, hoping for the best.

After the big explosion, after the lights
go down inside the house and up the street,
we rush outdoors to find a squirrel stopped
in straws of half-gnawed cable. I explain,
trying to fit the facts, "The squirrel is dead."

No, you explain it otherwise to me.
"He's sleeping. And his mommy going to come."
Later, when the squirrel has been removed,
"His mommy fix him," you insist, insisting
on the right to know what you believe.

The world is truly full of fabulous
great and curious small inhabitants,
and you're the freshly minted, unashamed
Adam in this garden. You preside,
appreciate, and judge our proper names.

Like God, I brought you here.
Like God, I seem to be omnipotent,
mostly helpful, sometimes angry as hell.
I fix whatever minor faults arise
with bandaids, batteries, masking tape, and pills.

But I am powerless, as you must know,
to chase the serpent sliding in the grass,
or the tall angel with the flaming sword
who scares you when he rises suddenly
behind the gates of sunset.

THE LAST OF THE COURTYARD

Who will believe me later, when I say
we lived in a state of music? Passing birds
and mice met on the roof, and danced away.

Francis played his silver flute, and Guy
his violin; the children sang in words.
Who will believe me later, when I say

we lived on little else from day to day?
Life in the courtyard was its own reward.
Mice danced across the roof, and ran away.

Carpenter, painter, potter: poverty
is the sole good a singing man affords,
though not at last sufficient. As they say,

we lose the things for which we cannot pay;
our houses were sold out, over our heads.
Even the dancing mice must go away,

nothing remains of us but memory,
a fleeting minor air, absently heard.
Who will believe me later, when I say
the mice danced on the roof, and ran away?

LEGACIES

Aunt Annie said, "When I turned seventeen,
old enough to take the train alone,
I went back to Detroit, and the big house
my father had abandoned, where my mother
Anna Sanger died of scarlet fever
when she was only thirty, eight months pregnant,
trying in vain to carry

his baby to term and leaving three small children.
He shipped us to his mother in the east,
locked the doors behind him, never returned.

"The house was sacked by loose acquaintances,
renters, mice, and brave nocturnal children
who spattered candle wax
on sills of jimmied windows, up the stairs.
All the satin drapes had long since rotted.
Nothing was left but sheet music and letters
(I took them home), the fruit-and-basket love seat
that you and I refinished and revived,
Father's bookshelves with their leaded glass,
handsome but much too heavy to bring back.

"I searched the rooms for traces of my mother,
but found only those polished memories
I'd counted over and over every evening
when I was four, and suddenly far from home.
I know I have her laugh,
and probably her temper. When her brother
came home to die years later, he bequeathed
pawn tickets to us, and a fur he claimed
was hers. Except the monogram was wrong,
and in its empty sleeves, the wrong perfume."

MARILYN HACKER
MEDITATING FORMALLY

The choice and use of a fixed or structured form—whether I learned it or invented it—has always been, for me, one of the primary pleasures of writing poetry. I have no political or aesthetic rationale for it, except that I like it. The intersection of that very sensory/sensual satisfaction, related to music, related to walking, breathing, all the rhythmic bodily motions, and the emotional or intellectual difficulty, complexity, of the narrative, lyric or meditative treatment of certain subjects creates a tension that is, for me, a mental equivalent of those physical states where pleasure approaches pain, or pain, pleasure—whether the activity involved is sex or hiking. I've never formally meditated, but I suspect the process is similar to what I've just described, indeed, as "meditating formally." Here, though, the focus of heightened awareness is language, and the multiple purposes of meaning, music and modulation it serves. I experience the same heightened interest and involvement as a reader of metrically structured poetry: an initial and a continued impetus for writing that way myself.

When I see a young (or not-so-young) writer counting syllables on her fingers, or marking stresses for a poem she's writing, or one she's reading, I'm pretty sure we'll have something in common, whatever our other differences may be.

EIGHT DAYS IN APRIL

1.

I broke a glass, got bloodstains on the sheet:
hereafter, must I only write you chaste
connubial poems? Now that I have traced
a way from there to here across the sweet-
est morning, rose-blushed blonde, will measured feet
advance processionally, where before
they scuff-heeled flights of stairs, kicked at a door,
or danced in wing-tips to a dirty beat?
Or do I tell the world that I have got
rich quick, got lucky (got laid), got just what
the doctor ordered, more than I deserved?
This is the second morning I woke curved
around your dreaming. In one night, I've seen
moonset and sunrise in your lion's mane.

2.

Moons set and suns rise in your lion's mane
through LP kisses or spread on my thighs.
Winter subsided while I fantasized
what April dawns frame in the windowpane.
Sweetheart, I'm still not getting enough sleep,
but I'm not tired, and outside it's spring
in which we sprang the afternoon shopping
after I'd been inside you, O so deep
I thought we would be tangled at the roots.
I think we are. (I've never made such noise.
I've never come so hard, or come so far
in such a short time.) You're an exemplar
piss-elegance is not reserved for boys.
Tonight we'll go out in our gangster suits.

3.

Last night we went out in our gangster suits,
but just across the street to Santerello's,
waited past nine for wine. We shone; the fellows
noticed. "You have a splendid linen coat,"
Dimitri told you as he sat us down.
(This used to be my local; now it's chic.)
A restaurant table's like a bed: we speak
the way we do calmed after love, alone
in the dark. There's a lot to get to know.
We felt bad; we felt better. Soon I was
laid back enough to drink around the bend.
You got me home, to bed, like an old friend.
I like you, Rachel, when you're scared, because
you tough it out while you're feeling it through.

4.

You tough it out while you're feeling it through:
sometimes the bed's rocked over tidal waves
that aren't our pleasures. Everyone behaves
a little strangely when they're in a new
neighborhood, language, continent, time zone.
We got here fast; your jet lag's worse than mine.
I only had Paris to leave behind.
You left your whole young history. My own
reminds me to remind you, waking shaken
with tears, dream-racked, is standard for the course.
We need accommodation that allows
each one some storage space for her dead horse.
If the title weren't already taken,
I'd call this poem "Directions to My House."

5.

I'd call this poem "Directions to My House,"
except today I'm writing it in yours,
in your paisley PJ's. The skylight pours
pale sunlight on white blankets. While I douse
my brain with coffee, you sleep on. Dream well
this time. We'll have three sets of keys apiece:
uptown, downtown, Paris on a sublease.
Teach me to drive. (Could I teach you to spell?)
I think the world's our house. I think I built
and furnished mine with space for you to move
through it, with me, alone in rooms, in love
with our work. I moved into one mansion
the morning when I touched, I saw, I felt
your face blazing above me like a sun.

6.

Your face blazing above me like a sun-
deity, framed in red-gold flames, *gynandre*
in the travail of pleasure, urgent, tender
terrible—my epithalamion
circles that luminous intaglio
—and you under me as I take you there,
and you opening me in your mouth where
the waves inevitably overflow
restraint. No, no, that isn't the whole thing
(also you drive like cop shows, and you sing
gravel and gold, are street-smart, book-smart,
laugh from your gut) but it is (a soothing
poultice applied to my afflicted part)
the central nervous system and the heart.

7.

The central nervous system and the heart,
and whatever it is in me wakes me
at 5 A.M. regardless, and what takes me
(when you do) ineluctably apart
and puts me back together; the too-smart,
too-clumsy kid glutted on chocolate cakes (me
at ten); the left-brain righteousness that makes me
make of our doubled dailiness an art
are in your capable square hands. O sweet,
possessives make me antsy: we are free
to choose each other perpetually.
Though I don't think my French short-back-and-sides
means I'll be the most orthodox of brides,
I broke a glass, got bloodstains on the sheet.

BALLAD OF LADIES LOST AND FOUND
for Julia Alvarez

Where are the women who, *entre deux guerres,*
came out on college-graduation trips,
came to New York on football scholarships,
came to town meeting in a decorous pair?
Where are the expatriate *salonnières,*
the gym teacher, the math-department head?
Do nieces follow where their odd aunts led?
The elephants die off in Cagnes-sur-Mer.
H.D., whose "nature was bisexual,"
and plain old Margaret Fuller died as well.

Where are the single-combat champions:
the Chevalier d'Eon with curled peruke,
Big Sweet who ran with Zora in the jook,
open-handed Winifred Ellerman,

Colette, who hedged her bets and always won?
Sojourner's sojourned where she need not pack
decades of whitegirl conscience on her back.
The spirit gave up Zora; she lay down
under a weed-field miles from Eatonville,
and plain old Margaret Fuller died as well.

Where's Stevie, with her pleated schoolgirl dresses,
and Rosa, with her permit to wear pants?
Who snuffed Clara's *mestiza* flamboyance
and bled Frida onto her canvases?
Where are the Niggerati hostesses,
the kohl-eyed ivory poets with severe
chignons, the rebels who grew out their hair,
the bulldaggers with marcelled processes?
Conglomerates co-opted Sugar Hill,
and plain old Margaret Fuller died as well.

Anne Hutchinson, called witch, termagant, whore
fell to the long knives, having tricked the noose.
Carolina Maria de Jesús'
tale from the slagheaps of the landless poor
ended on a straw mat on a dirt floor.
In action thirteen years after fifteen
in prison, Eleanor of Aquitaine
accomplished half of Europe and fourscore
anniversaries for good or ill,
and plain old Margaret Fuller died as well.

Has Ida B. persuaded Susan B.
to pool resources for a joint campaign?
(Two Harriets act a pageant by Lorraine,
cheered by the butch drunk on the IRT
who used to watch me watch her watching me;
We've notes by Angelina Grimké Weld
for choral settings drawn from the *Compiled*

Poems of Angelina Weld Grimké.)
There's no such tense as Past Conditional,
and plain old Margaret Fuller died as well.

Who was Sappho's protégée, and when did
we lose Hrotsvitha, dramaturge and nun?
What did bibulous Suzanne Valadon
think about Artemisia, who tended
to make a life-size murderess look splendid?
Where's Aphra, fond of dalliance and the pun?
Where's Jane, who didn't indulge in either one?
Whoever knows how Ende, Pintrix, ended
is not teaching Art History at Yale,
and plain old Margaret Fuller died as well.

Is Beruliah upstairs behind the curtain
debating Juana Inés de la Cruz?
Where's *savante* Anabella, Augusta-Goose,
Fanny, Maude, Lidian, Freda and Caitlin,
"without whom this could never have been written"?
Louisa who wrote, scrimped, saved, sewed, and
    nursed,
Malinche, who's, like all translators, cursed,
Bessie, whose voice was hemp and steel and satin,
outside a segregated hospital,
and plain old Margaret Fuller died as well.

Where's Amy, who kept Ada in cigars
and love, requited, both country and courtly,
although quinquagenarian and portly?
Where's Emily? It's very still upstairs.
Where's Billie, whose strange fruit ripened in bars?
Where's the street-scavenging Little Sparrow?
Too poor, too mean, too weird, too wide, too narrow:
Marie Curie, examining her scars,
was not particularly beautiful;
and plain old Margaret Fuller died as well.

Who was the grandmother of Frankenstein?
The Vindicatrix of the Rights of Woman.
Madame de Sévigné said prayers to summon
the postman just as eloquent as mine,
though my Madame de Grignan's only nine.
But Mary Wollstonecraft had never known
that daughter, nor did Paula Modersohn.
The three-day infants blinked in the sunshine.
The mothers turned their faces to the wall;
and plain old Margaret Fuller died as well.

Tomorrow night the harvest moon will wane
that's floodlighting the silhouetted wood.
Make your own footnotes; it will do you good.
Emeritae have nothing to explain.
She wasn't very old, or really plain—
my age exactly, volumes incomplete.
"The life, the life, will it never be sweet?"
She wrote it once; I quote it once again
midlife at midnight when the moon is full
and I can almost hear the warning bell
offshore, sounding through starlight like a stain
on waves that heaved over what she began
and truncated a woman's chronicle,
and plain old Margaret Fuller died as well.

DUSK: JULY

Late afternoon rain of a postponed summer:
wet streets, wet slate roofs, swish of tires, wet
    awnings,
pin-curled neighbor leaning out on her wrought-iron
window-guard, smoking,

wet chestnuts, wet lavender by the river's
shades of gray-green. This over-subtle season

will not burst, all clarity, into sunlight.
Petal by petal,

tiger-lilies open up in a pitcher,
orange, yellow, stars or beast-faces yawning.
Leaves like feast-day offerings round an altar
drop on the carpet.

I would love my love, but my love is elsewhere.
I would take a walk with her in the evening's
milky pearl. I'd sleep with my arms around her
confident body,

arms and legs asprawl like an adolescent.
We're not adolescents. Our friends are dying
and between us nothing at all is settled
except our loving.

We've loved other bodies the years have altered:
knuckles swollen, skin slackened, eyelids grainy;
bodies that have gone back to earth, the synapse
of conscience broken.

Softly, softly, speak of it, but say something.
We are middle-aged and our friends are dying.
What do we lie down beside when we lie down
alone, together?

If I could remember the names, the places,
rooms and faces, gestures and conversations,
I'd have some excuse for the years passed through me
like air, like water:

school friends who turned into suburban matrons;
bar friends, one-night-stands, who are dead of AIDS, or
tenured, or in jail, or suburban matrons;
great-aunts, grandparents

of whom I had nothing to tell my daughter.
Those dead Jews on both sides of the Atlantic
disappear again as the year two thousand
washes us under.

Seize the days, the days, or the years will seize them,
leaving just the blink of a burnt-out lightbulb
with a shard of filament left inside that
ticks when it's shaken.

Fix the days in words and the years will seize them
anyway: a bracket of dates, an out-of-
print book, story nobody told, rooms locked and
phone disconnected,

cemetery no one will ever visit.
Who knows where my grandparents' graves are?
    Who cut
through the gauze unveiling my mother's tombstone?
I don't. I didn't.

Light is still alive in the table-lamp I
switch on in the nine o'clock twilight; music
still alive in street noise; mine one more shadow
drawing the curtains.

I just want to wake up beside my love who
wakes beside me. One of us will die sooner;
one of us is going to outlive the other,
but we're alive now.

RACHEL HADAS
THE SKILLS OF THE STOW-AWAY

I began writing imitative poems by the time I was
nine or ten—I can remember, with embarrassment, a
balladish piece about wee bairns being put to bed. By
thirteen, like countless other young people, I was ap-
ing e.e. cummings; around the same time there was
also a fake-medieval ballad about the Crucifixion, and,
a little later, scores of Shakespearean sonnets, some in
more or less Elizabethan guise, some in accents closer
to Meredith's *Modern Love*. Nothing is quite as world-
weary as a fifteen-year-old.

A year or so later, at the end of high school and the
beginning of college, I was starting to write poems I
now regard as juvenilia but not absolute pastiche: "Super
Nivem," "The Fall of Troy," "After the Cave," and—
after my father's death—"That Time, This Place," and
"Daddy." The best of these poems (many of which are
collected in my first book, *Starting from Troy*) feel less
like imitations than like imaginative syntheses of my
reading and experience. I had no one model for any of
them, and superficially speaking I made up my forms
(the three-line stanzas of "Super Nivem" or the syllabics
of "Ode") as I went along. But iambic pentameter was
ringing in my ears, together with dactylic hexameter,
Sapphics, Alcaics: I had four years of Latin (the best
of it studying Vergil) in high school and started Greek
in college.

The point is not that at a given hour I said "I'll write
like Tibullus/Propertius/Catullus/Archilochus"—though

translating the odd fragment didn't hurt. But I understood fairly early on that originality, in poetry, is a highly relative term. All writing is rewriting—something like this was my first crude formulation of the idea John Hollander puts much more elegantly: writing, far from being easier than reading (as beginning poets often think), is instead a difficult *form* of reading. Thus in a course on Roman elegy I came across the Greek term *paraclausithyron*, a generic term for a lament sung before the locked door of the beloved. Of course I made the term mine by writing my own *paraclausithyron*, with a certain suite in Harvard's Adams House in mind.

Wherever poems come from and wherever it is they fly off to, the young poet, and then the not-so-young poet, needs some of the skills of the stow-away: to climb aboard the vehicle, to make use of it to get you where you want to go. Is the vehicle formal verse technique? I'd rather call it all the poems ever written before—and having said that I realize I'm echoing a favorite passage of mine from Robert Frost, so—moving from aeronautics to meteorology—I'll let him have the last word:

> No one given to looking underground in spring can have failed to notice how a bean starts its growth from the seed. Now the manner of a poet's germination is less like that of a bean in the ground than of a water-spout at sea. He [sic] has to begin as a cloud of all the other poets he ever read. That can't be helped. And first the cloud reaches down toward the water from above and then the water reaches up toward the cloud from below and finally cloud and water join together to roll as one pillar between heaven and earth. The base of water he picks up from below is of course all the life he ever lived outside of books.

THE HOUSE BESIDE THE SEA

I wore that fiction like a fine white shirt
And asked no favor but to play the part.
                                    —James Merrill

Like a fine *what* shirt I put it on,
the house beside the sea,
enclosing like a tangy honeymoon
the fiction of a place for you and me?

   A fine white shirt.

White? Without my eyes I couldn't see.
I merely felt the shining of the sea.
I have no eyes or teeth, but I can hear.
Are those gigantic scissors near my ear?

   Snip. Snip. Snip. Lock hell.

Hell is locked out, I know it. Thank you, though.
No one is here in this salt bungalow
but me, I think. And you? Could you be there,
swathed in the sheer white scrim of ever after?

   Snip. Snip. Snip.

It takes no eyes to sense
something is cutting at the final thread
that ties us two together,
keeps me near the salt blood of the sea.

   Lock hell.

The house that locks hell out,
the house hell locks me into,
the house of hell? And yet
I'm glad to be alive here.

   Snip. Snip. Snip.

No eyes, no taste,
only ablution (Keats's reverie
of pure ablution round earth's human shores)
or threadbare fabric of another day;

   a fine white shirt

clutched at and held, survival's jagged tear,
the house beside the sea,
the radiance of vestments,
rags of the robe unravelling in salt air.

WINGED WORDS

Trying to speak means flailing with
gestures half-sculpted out of need,
eloquent in the way of myth:
monumental, hard to read.
How does anything get said?
A nascent, feebly struggling thought,
hard to collect and to recover,
contrives to spit its substance out.
Words are the wings that lift us over.

Garbling a recollected tongue,
swamped in simultaneity,
latecome words go down among
syllables learned by the age of three.
Look light kitty love you me—
for every flight from the teeth's gate,
as Homer has it, others are
prisoners, crying "let us out,
out of this dumbness, away from here!"

See me, poised and ready for
writing the words that cluster round.
My moving pen is an open door

releasing symbol into sound.
Sprung from dumbness by my hand,
a few words fly. By some stern law
of choice or chance the empty air
fills—with what I scarcely know.
Writing it down might make it clear.

Words are flighty. But once set down,
utterances give form to life,
celebrate pleasure, focus pain.
Every writer wields a knife
sharp with danger. Nothing's safe.
When offered up to clarity,
memory acquires mysterious power.
With each i dotted and each crossed t,
intimate histories appear.

Is it for love of you I read
your sentences as points of pain,
or does attention always breed
phantoms of meaning like a stain?
Show me that page you wrote again.
Now I sense an undertow
tugging you far away from here.
What you felt and saw and knew
sticks to the paper like a scar.

A child is curled in his mother's arm.
The lamplight page or hammock's sway
create a zone exempt from harm,
devoted to one kind of play.
Dream all night and read all day.
Tell it again, the precious tale
of what we lose, seek, reacquire.
Sunset again. The sky goes pale.
A great page flickers with words of fire.

Eye usurps mind and mouth. Exclusion
of idle chat holds death at bay.

Silence allows no clear conclusion
except she has no more to say.
Today's no different from yesterday.
Read her the news; or improvise,
when you can bear to read no more,
some speech that needs no lips or eyes.
Conversation is metaphor.

The lips are locked. What else is left?
I can no longer read the gaze.
Pity for a life bereft
of power to tell, amuse, amaze...
Reduced to stillness, year-long days
pass in a fog of who can tell?
I'd say the password's *Nevermore.*
Other conclusions loom as well.
What was language ever for?

All we have done, all we will do—
helplessly we write and read,
opening the veins of what we know.
Even when pain is understood
the mildest scribble may draw blood.
Why does the dark authority
of written language reassure?
This fearful self is more than me.
Our words are bodies. We write on air.

Words are the wings that lift us over
out of this limbo, away from here.
Writing it down might make it clear.
Intimate histories appear,
stick to the paper like a scar.
A great page flickers with words of fire.
Conversation is metaphor.
What was language ever for?
Our words are bodies. We write on air.

THE LAIR

Excess of lemon, whether on the phone
or just inside my head:
that mind's mean eye.

Walking this afternoon I was alone;
saw harmless people fishing by the brook
and had to force myself to smile a Hi.

Kept walking. Passed. We're each of us alone.
Light flickers from a frayed electric switch.
Ever so softly rain

starts on the roof. They're all asleep but me.
I do not have to smile at anyone.
I chew my gum, write down uncharity.

Writing to B. tonight, my courage failed.
I had been going to send her something I
wrote about her and me three years ago.

Who'd give by now a rusty fuck if not
she—or she least of all? I threw my hands
up, filled the letter with mild pleasantry,

left out the point, the poem. Everything
sticks, gummed *esprit* on the *escalier*,
what one only now takes heart to say

under the blanket Night.
A manticore twitches its stinging tail.
Visions curl together out of light.

JOSEPHINE JACOBSEN
BASIC RHYTHMS

I am happy to see so many good evidences of the "New Formalism," never having abandoned the old. As I wrote poems of a non-formal structure in the relatively rare instances in which it seemed to me that that was what the specific poem required, so I continued to write poems of a varied formalness during a prolonged period when this was, in many quarters, deemed totally unacceptable—and managed to survive, poetically speaking.

I have always felt that the various aspects of formalism gave the poet his or her best opportunity for the struggle and tension which the creation of a poem should involve. I have great belief in basic rhythms—breath, tides, seasons, music, incantation, Yeats' preoccupation with the dance.

I am, in general, a bit suspicious of all trends, and am happy in formalism chiefly because I think it renews the exploration of that rhythm which musicians, athletes, and scientists daily experience.

ONLY ALICE

entered that brilliant intimate
room; you cannot, ever, pick
the grapes whose luster mounds the plate
or hear that gilt French clock tick.

Will not smell the red roses, ever,
taste, touch or hear. Only your eyes

watch eyes which see the face you never
will. That room is silent with surprise

and lure of inaccessible terrain.
The gilded frame surrounds a whole
of something present that explains
the old belief that it can snatch a soul.

It shows no welcome, and no malice,
ambiguous as any Mona Lisa.
You are outside. There is no talis-
man; no passport and no visa.

So stare and stay; so stare, beguiled
and balked. And there's the matter
of luck, should you know—like a furious child—
that what you may not enter, you can shatter.

THE LIMBO DANCER

No limbo this week. Or next. Now it turns out
the limbo dancer is dead. Tiles between sea
and bar are clean for the guests' uncertain feet
that search the band's racket for how they should
    move.
The sea is dark and those rungs of the moon's fire
lead nowhere; but broken and bright the ladder lies.

The limbo dancer had nutmeg-colored feet
with apricot-colored heels, and toes splayed out
inch and half-inch. The guests could barely see
that motion grip the tiles. And how can a man move
inch after half-inch, as his body lies
horizontal on air? In his teeth he carried fire.

When the rod was high (and there was no fire
yet) the limbo dancer addressed it: his feet

shifted in place, his pelvis jumped in, and out,
and the light from the sequins and sweat, that flies
over ribs, showed how bone and muscle move.
His eyes shone too, at whatever they managed to see.

The pans, sweet and metallic, that sent out
a torrent, hushed; and the dark drum, four feet
high, spoke, as the rod dropped into its last move.
The limbo dancer, tall, taller than drums, Watusi-
tall, beaten forward inch by inch, as inch relies
on inch-space, moved, moved: toes, heels, and fire.

Whatever more liquidly indifferent than the sea?
But the guests, diverted from rum and drawn by fire,
stared, as the head came under, and the great feet
shot up, the limbo dancer's flame put out
in his mouth's cavern. For a shocked space, the move
was into that joy where gravity's laws are lies.

The limbo dancer, together with his feet,
has disappeared, and the guests are put out.
In shadows, on sand, by the noisy sea,
the old foe gravity (plane, bird, poem) lies
in wait. If that stretched body fails to move,
who will kill gravity by inches, spring up, eat fire?

The limbo dancer's fire is certainly out.
The guests say, See, alas, he does not move.
But gravity lies beneath the dust of his feet.

LENORE KEESHIG-TOBIAS
An Ancient Technique

Repetition connects my poetry with the oral tradition. I'm Native, so that's my background. I refused to study English literature in university, even though I write in English, even though most First Nations write in English. Instead I studied on my own, reading other Native authors. I felt safer with that, because they had already done a lot of the work of sifting out what was irrelevant to our way of expression.

I have spent a long time developing an understanding of the technique of oral storytelling and its purpose. I am a storyteller; poetry to me is just a style, a way of storytelling. Our people say that storytellers are teachers. They say that mother is the first teacher. As storytellers we have to realize that our stories have an impact on people—the people who hear or read us as well as the people the stories are about. The storyteller must take responsibility for that. I expect that people will learn from the content of the poems, but also from the form. From the form, they'll learn about traditional storytelling, and also about nurturing.

Repetition takes place in a number of ways in the oral tradition—repetition of sounds, words, incidents and events. To me it's very important; it's a teaching device. Words on paper are like recipes in a cookbook—writing to me is just a memory technique. It would be nice if I could create wampum or something to record my stories, but instead they're in words on a page.

With the repetition in "Mother with Child," I was

also thinking of the repetition that takes place in nurturing. When I was brushing my children's hair, I would feel like my mother brushing my hair—and my mother told me she remembered the same feeling from being with her mother. And when you're encouraging someone to be brave and courageous, not to be afraid to do something, you need to use repetition. The repetition in this poem is about the subject of mother and child and the continuousness of mothering.

It was only after the university, when I started reading traditional narratives and listening to oral technique, that it began to click in my mind that I had been doing the same thing unconsciously and that other Native writers had been doing it too. Since I have become more aware of traditional techniques in storytelling, it has given my work more validity, to know that I am using an ancient technique. But I try not to overdo it; I use repetition just enough to create a nice tension. The skill comes in recognizing when not to overdo it.

I GREW UP

I

i grew up on the reserve
thinking it was the most
beautiful place in the world

i grew up thinking
i'm never going
to leave this place

i was a child
a child who would
lie under trees

watching wind's rhythms
sway leafy boughs
back and forth

back and forth
sweeping it seemed
the clouds into great piles

and rocking me as
i snuggled in the grass
like a bug basking in the sun

II

i grew upon the reserve
thinking it was the most
beautiful place in the world

i grew up thinking
i'm never going
to leave this place

i was a child
a child who ran
wild rhythms

through the fields
the streams
the bush

eating berries
cupping cool water
to my wild stained mouth

and hiding in the
treetops with
my friends

III

we used to laugh at teachers and
tourists who referred to
our bush as *forest* or *woods*

forests and *woods*
were places of
fairy-tale text

were places where people,
especially children, got lost
where wild beasts roamed

our bush was where we played
and where the rabbits squirrels
foxes deer and the bear lived

i grew up thinking
*i'm never going to
leave this place*

i grew up on the reserve
thinking it was the most
beautiful place in the world

MOTHER WITH CHILD

Oh Mother, so many times
i would sit on
i would sit on
that kitchen chair

with the night's sleep
or an afternoon of play
tangled in my hair

and you with your
tummy full of child
tummy full of child
would nudge nudge and press

against my shoulders
against my shoulders
against my back

soothing my wildness
while combing my hair
while combing my hair

DOLORES KENDRICK
ON THE CRAFT OF POEMS

I see Poetry as an art form, and, like most art forms,
it has its own discipline and its own demands. What-
ever we refer to when we call into being "The Muse"
usually is at the center of such form and is simply
awaiting the poet's permission to go ahead, so to speak,
take the risk, follow, produce that word or phrase that
might otherwise sound strange within a "normal" con-
text, see where it takes you, challenge the fear that
lurks in what we like to think of as rationality, and
move to that other level of creativity of which we know
so little, but which has proved itself over and over
again as the source of all creativity, and which is rarely,
if ever, in error; that creativity which at once becomes
a source of power and impunity: the imagination as
matter unresolved.

We poets are the children of such imagination, a com-
post reality that most of us are invited to, some of us
enter, some of us shun. But that reality is at the heart
of our craft, the knowledge of which should, at least,
keep us humble. To do it justice we should apply our
craft as any other artist would, refining, sculpting, be-
coming increasingly careful of not only what we say,
but also of how we say it. Otherwise we may have
"recollected in tranquility" what may not at all be tranquil.

SOLO: THE GOOD BLUES
(for Alberta Hunter)

long way from the whorehouse
to the White House
long song long gone
gone when I was twelve
stretching to thirteen
stretching to thirty,
fifty, long eighty

> *ain't no whorehouse*
> *can hold a holy girl*
> *ain't no whorehouse*
> *can hold a holy girl*
> *it's the song that matters*
> *nothing else in this world*

get me to Paris
get me a name
get me (if you can)
in the long note game!

tell me your trouble
tell me your sin
just call me Woman
I'm your next-of-kin:

write off the lonely
write off the sad
my dream's a hurtin'
my sorrow's had!

ain't no whorehouse
can hold a holy girl
ain't no whorehouse
can hold a holy girl
it's the song that matters
nothing else in this world

wide way from the whorehouse
to the White House
wide from girl to Woman
deep and wide from little
Black girls who had a song
but nowhere to sing it
except whorehouses
long and deep and wide

thank you, mr. president,
my, this house is big,
it almost fills my throat!

my God! What a morning!

my long Black God!
we made it! and I'm
the living proof!

hold the holy, hold the holy girl
hold the holy, hold the holy girl
take her in an octave
and give her to the world.

NOTE TO THE OPHTHALMOLOGIST

The apparatus is right:
It gleams properly flushing
Now into the night
Room that shines through seams

Of my eyeballs; screams
Of darkness don't matter:
Remember that. Whatever leans
Out of this eye is refuse

And prayer, the juice
Of retina poured from images
Only. The steely obtuse
Conversation between

Doesn't help at all. I mean
You Ophthalmologists are so helpless
After all. The best you glean
From my unclothed eye

Is sight; vision is high,
Too strong and deep for the big machine:
But instruments and scientists don't lie
And my hyperopia is a gift.

What is distance now is sift
From light, draining my gut (and backward).
Distance is liquid myopia, a lift
Into metals, forms, images, cold.

The eye of the storm
Is the window of my soul.

GETHSEMANE A.D.

The Garden did not bloom
that year. It tossed its roots
into the open moon
emptied like shoots

of sunflowers drained from
a man's blood, sticking his eyes

until the rose that did not come
ached upon his mouth. The lies

were not his. (How could they be?)
They moved into the earth
like worms feeding tree to tree
changing death to birth.

The Man is gone, the Garden wide
awake with soothsayers' stones,
and if here a young man slightly died,
wept blood, offered bones

of his imagination to a kiss,
then blooms are out of place;
tomorrow he will ripe and rise,
release the terrible energy of his grace.

WE ARE THE WRITING ON THE WALL

We are the writing on the wall
our Black dynasties of blood
running into stone

the young alphabet of our grief
stronger than the whines of citizenry
stalking us alone

with nostrils wide like pumas
pacing their impatient properties.
We are the bone

of that daylight squatting in the dark
sealed in the absolution of tombs;
the hieroglyphic home.

JANE KENYON
SHIELDING

Two of these three poems were written while I was recovering from my father's death. I don't know what made me turn to formal verse at that time, but I found that in having to concentrate on the metrics I was shielded in some way from the content of the poems.

TRAVEL: AFTER A DEATH

We drove past farms, the hills terraced with sheep.
A rook flapped upward from the stubbled corn;
its shadow fell across my lap one instant
and then was gone. The car was warm. Sleepy,
we passed through Devonshire: sun and showers....
Fields, emerald in January, shone
through leafless hedges, and I watched a man
grasping his plaid cloth cap and walking stick
in one hand, while with perfect courtesy
he sent his dog before him through the stile,
bowing a little like a maître d'.

We found a room in a cold seaside hotel.
The manager had left a sullen girl
—no more than eighteen—and a parakeet
to run his business while he sunned himself
in Portugal. We watched her rip the key
from the wall and fling it toward us. Why,
I wondered, was the front door wedged open
in January, with a raw sea wind
blowing the woolen skirts of the townswomen,
who passed with market baskets on their arms,
their bodies bent forward against the chill
and the steep angle of the cobbled hill?

There were two urns of painted porcelain
flanking the door. A man could stand in one
and still have room for ashes... though he'd have
to be a strange man, like the poet Donne,
who pulled a shroud around himself and called
someone to draw—from life—his deathbed scene;
or like Turgenev, who saw bones and skulls
instead of Londoners walking the streets....
Oh, when am I going to own my mind again?

INPATIENT

The young attendants wrapped him in a red
velour blanket, and pulled the strapping taut.
Sedated on a stretcher and outside
for the last time, he raised his head and sniffed
the air like an animal. A wedge of geese
flew honking over us. The sky leaned close;
a drop of rain fell on his upturned face.
I stood aside, steward of Grandma's red-
letter New Testament and an empty vase.
The nurse went with him through the sliding door.
Without having to speak of it we left
the suitcase with his streetclothes in the car.

ALONE FOR A WEEK

I washed a load of clothes
and hung them out to dry.
Then I went up to town
and busied myself all day.
The sleeve of your best shirt
rose ceremonious

when I drove in; our night-
clothes twined and untwined in
a little gust of wind.

For me it was getting late;
for you, where you were, not.
The harvest moon was full
but sparse clouds made its light
not quite reliable.
The bed on your side seemed
as wide and flat as Kansas;
your pillow plump, cool,
and allegorical....

MARY KINZIE
Some Thoughts on the Threshold of Form and the Level of Words

We give the name of poet to somone who can keep
taut the many threads out of which the literary work
must be woven, while passing through these a shuttle
of thematic and formal tenor that varies from poem to
poem. I find it helpful to distinguish six elements out
of which poems are composed: line, sentence, diction,
trope, argument (voice), and rhythm. As a rule, only
one or two of these are made to shift, while the others
are maintained by the poet on a sort of plateau. Con-
sequently, all the elements must be acknowledged, and
managed, by being either carefully suspended within
the weave, or by striking variation, in order for the
poem to attain a suitable artistic threshold. In other
words, below this threshold of alert, conscious, *con-
certed* control, the work may be pleasing as journalism
or rhetoric, but not as art.

The line, originally auditory, is now increasingly a
visual and typographic measure, controlling the reader's
experience of interval and time. It can also control our
experience of logic. This occurs because the line is al-
ways augmented or partially negated by the competi-
tive presence of the syntax. Line either coincides with
the sentence, or tugs against it. Certain patterns of co-
incidence or tension occur within certain sentences in
certain sorts of lines. The simpler and more declara-
tive the syntax, the briefer the statements and hence
the greater the tendency, when sentences are simple,
to make the lines coincident with them, until the end

of the line invariably coincides with the end of a phrase or thought. By contrast, complex, subordinating syntax will implicate longer segments of the line and involve a greater chance of enjambment (run-over).

Keeping this loose bundle of ideas in mind helps when one begins to think about (let us say) trope. Consider the types of trope, or metaphor, from the simplest and most casual comparative hypothesis ("O my luve's like a red, red rose") to the nearly syllogistic loopings in "That time of year thou mayst in me behold/When..."; the more involute the metaphor, the longer the sentence needed to elaborate it, and hence the more the line will tend to be swallowed by the sentence (as, indeed, we find in the three sentence-long quatrains of Shakespeare's seventy-third sonnet).

Or consider how the tension-or-coincidence idea where line and sentence are concerned clarifies the role of *diction* in a poem. A term that implies the thematic as well as the stylistic level of an utterance, diction is instantly and profoundly affected by the length of the poetic line. If the lines are short and end-stopped, the diction will tend to be monosyllabic and concrete. Polysyllabism within brief lines sounds hieratic or gnomic. It is impossible to produce an expansive, discursive, and conversational utterance if the polysyllabic diction proper to it is closed in short lines. This rule of thumb is owing to the fact that, strung together, polysyllabic words *eat up* the lines, ensuring that, at most, we can navigate a phrase, but not a completed predication, in the space of a line (consider Wordsworth's line "Of all this unintelligible world"—the modification of an idea that is neither the subject nor the predicate of the fourteen-and-a-half-line sentence in which it occurs—as contrasted with Donne's "I dare not move my dim eyes any way"—a sentence at once dramatically complete, and virtually monosyllabic, cohering within one line of iambic pentameter).

When we talk about *rhythm,* we talk about nothing more nor less than the way in which the poem plaits together (but never quite evenly) these very threads of diction, sentence, line, rhetorical stance, and metaphoricity (the metaphoricity that so contributes to a sense of boundaries blurring between states of being, or forms of saying). Many poets elect a numerical or even temporal measure as well, a choice that complicates the poem's rhythm and produces a denser music and more subtle fingering. But even free verse poems have, acknowledge, and use *rhythm* in this extended sense.

I might briefly illustrate the idea of overall style or rhythm by reference to a stylistic choice in my own work involving blank verse (unrhymed iambic pentameter with occasional—and necessary—enjambment). Blank verse is the verse form I have used more often than any other. Many of the *Autumn Eros* poems as well as the four central poems in my book *Summers of Vietnam* are written in it, but the sense, sound, and entire affect of each differs. "Ringing Words" is a blank-verse poem in which the speaker excoriates herself and her protected milieu for evasion. The syntax is formally (and emotionally) headlong, bitter, aggressive, the many line boundaries always differently rounded or navigated, with frequent touches of irregularity and over-stressing. In "Ringing Words," I have deliberately played with the over-rich bonding effect of alliterative patterns and have also explored the sudden, nightmare effect of a reduced line in an otherwise fully fleshed-out metre ("Feeding its stripes into the sea"). This last device (the reduced line) is even sharper in the rhymed stanza of "Boy."

My book *Autumn Eros* also explores the enormous variety of verse, from the audible extreme (I use a number of stanza forms in the book—rhyme royal in "Boy," the ballade of "Sound Waves," heroic couplets, rhyming stanzas of my own invention) to the forms we in our period now experience primarily as typographic and architectonic, blank verse and hexameter. I am conscious of trying to make certain forms do what they may not have been designed to. In each of the two suites of haiku, for example, I attempt to make eight closed haiku tell a story in metaphor (see "Canicula"), and I have disguised a poem in sapphics ("Sun and Moon") lest the consciousness of its archaic pedigree inhibit the conversational tempo. All of these pursue a different degree and kind of tension between verse line and sentence, the music of "Sun and Moon" being the most cadential.

Over time, I have become conscious of form as a threshold that must be crossed repeatedly, each time as if from the beginning. This path must be retraced by the critic and teacher, too. My hope for poetry in the time to come is that we can "train up" readers who are willing to pause at the level of words before deriving their interpretations. After all, this is where the music starts.

SUN AND MOON

Complements. Like figures in statuary
Gardens, his a cabled athletic pose, hers
A mermaid's slithering beyond the pool's lip,
    They employ difference

To define, play out such exaggerations
as *Water Floods Rock*. Each the other's private
Lightness tries to ground, or black weight help
   lighten,
     Acting the obverse.

Struggling to take shape, he contrives a drama
(*Rock Displacing Water*) of will, his *Too-Calm*
Brought to simmering by her permitted *Fire*.
   Fighting indifference,

Meticulous his study, its blazing page
Neat and thoughtful. Hers a rough centrifuge of
Clutter thrown out from the abject crescent where,
   Leaning on elbows,

Head in hand, she worries about his future
While he suffers old indignation. Thus they
Stiffen into orbit, for all their future
    Equal in exile.

What can have put them on this track where turning
Off is met by turning toward exactly?
Instability, which could not have fused them
    But at a distance?

Much more likely sentiment—hall umbrellas
Touching with a hesitant air, their questions
Nervous, soft, and forced—even their deference
    Coarsened by sadness

And remorse. The flesh at this hint more shrouded
Glimpses down the vista of itself stiff arms
Like tree limbs in rites so redundant they are
    Thought to lack magic.

Lurid as if scarred by a fire, their garden
Shines with punishment, while the simple planets
Crank about the sky manifesting signs of
   Knowledge and justice.

BOY

By day his world extends, far, knotted, hot.
Wasps long as fingers drag their jet black legs.
The concrete of the steps is cool but not
Cooling as a fine grit sticks to his legs.
How much he knows of them, no one suspects.
Mother is bathing. He is in her room,
Picks up a bottle filled with red perfume,

Red as his hair. The bottle like a spire
Thrusts toward the point of crystalline desire
Scattering rainbows on the mirror higher
Than he can touch. He does not try. Wire
Hangers whisper, curtains clasp the fire
The sun starts to pour downward on this side,
Which means a nap with his eyes open wide

And a hot fretfulness that is like fear
Brushing at the faint temples of his head.
The others are at school, but will appear
In strange unravellings of joy like thread,
Also mixed with dread.
Crossing the street in danger, down the block,
They will lift the shield of their majestic talk.

His mother comes out. She has put her robe
Around the baby she wears in her skin.
He may not climb against that living globe;
But with her cool arms she still draws him in
As if he were her boy, had always been.

They look among her bracelets for a toy
That might be helpful to a napping boy.

Inevitably, nothing is enough
To make up for her absence. The family rob
Him hourly of themselves until, weak, gruff,
He throws his hand out with a practice sob,
The bracelet bounding with a hollow throb—
Sounds that mingle like an overture
To blackness, solitude, and forfeiture.

He nearly suffocates in his defense.
He cannot get the whole out that he knows.
When he jumps to be free, there is the fence
Of his quick temper and his dirty clothes
And the ill-fated moment that he chose
To climb into the lap and claim that kiss.
His tantrum then just sets their prejudice.

Curious and fragile he slips through
The pattern of their futures like a ghost.
Unlike his actions, his door is not closed
So he can drift into his sister's room
When he can't sleep at night. What comforts most
Is being too good, waiting, as in play,
Then climbing up when she says that he may.

SOUND WAVES

I (*At fourteen weeks*)

In the first negative, a shape presages
The almost human profile of the skull
Against a bolster the technician gauges
Could be placenta. Like a general

Reposed in state—or like a fogbound hull—
The infant drifts among its dim debris
Of nourishment and rigging, a vehicle
Tethered to darkness by one spectral knee,
  Rib and feature faint in quality.

II (*At sixteen weeks*)

A fortnight later, hurtling through its stages
So fast the brow has doubled, the huge null
Of the eye socket—now twice as deep—engages
The parents' with its primal monocle
(The other eye blurred by some obstacle),
As if to caution us, or disagree.
What have we done? This enigmatical
Creature has spied our mediocrity,
  Rib and feature white with gravity.

III (*At twenty-one weeks*)

Seeming to speak, a fresh image assuages
That baleful hollow glare: A chronicle
Of kind floats forth and riffles through the pages
Of its movements. After an interval
With an arm upraised, to mark the body's lull,
Something like smiling flickers on the screen,
In recognition of its own sweet will
Buoyed above the molten vertebrae,
  Rib and feature warm with clemency.

Envoi

A second view looks from the fontanelle
Down through the shining oval cavity

Where thread is spun. The spine curves in this well
Like a rope dropped from the vertex to that sea
  Where rib and feature weave their history.

While in the last one, and most personal,
The feet we know as hers lie sleepily
Side by side, but not quite parallel.
Each is bird-like, or like a fluted shell,
Yet close to home, just as her self would be,
  And ribbed and featured with humanity.

CANICULA

Fireflies float noiseless
In the high, perturbing din
Of the late locust.

* * *

The orchard dying—
Trunks badged with disease lean down,
Tranquil in their thirst.

* * *

In air hard as sand,
Now the sun boils off to blue,
Moths sip from a leaf.

* * *

Heat-heavy creatures
Wake and feed on their diet
Of self and other.

* * *

Want, predation, sleep.
Often all of these at once
In nature; in dream.

* * *

Among mosquitoes
Their spears half clouding, blue spruce
Defend the portal.

* * *

Glinting like water
But incapable of touch,
Youth, its swift old strength.

* * *

But her arm—damp, small—
She is not part of the wheel...
Her pretty breathing.

RINGING WORDS

They have closed the prison where they had you
     teach
The killers no one else would touch. Brutal,
Mercurial, in lessons they would leap
Catlike in a twinkling to the desk
Or throw you to the ground and in distraction
Toy with you, half-sated tigers with
Unappetizing fare, but flanked by foes.

So the last casualties have followed you
Into a daylight too much for their eyes,
The wards and keeps flushed out in back of them.

If many stayed down, tormented by their boredom
To deeps of vehemence not to be calmed,
Bleeding mad, their babble like the birds',
Some died. The walls would crumble around them all.

"Forget," said the voice politic, "that place
Sacramental in the crime it fed
Even as it punished it. Our health
Requires this. Our. Our. My spared limbs
Tremble with a passion the old rue
Will punish later. "Some memorial
Is needed to appall the mind," I said,

"Lest all he had resisted when it mattered
Little any more, loosen like Proteus,
Shrug away its hides, and sink oblivious
To all its harm—yes, feeling the bright blood move,
The freshened sinews round the strengthened bone,
Feeding its stripes into the sea."

CAROLYN KIZER
A Defense of Breathing

Writing about the iambic pentameter is like writing a defense of breathing. When I was a child I had severe asthma. I would lie perfectly still and concentrate on the production of the next breath. So I have never since been able to take breathing for granted. It is both the most natural and the most concentrated activity I know. One breath and the pentameter line have the same duration.

Sometimes I believe that my students think that the iambic pentameter was thought up by a group of ancient scholars with long beards and imposed on the prosodic canon with malicious intent: those who don't obey it are not poets! Then one must remind them of the origins of poetry in prayer and dance: rhythmic activities. One of the problems of the modernized services of worship is that the old rhythms are destroyed by a group of men with tin ears who are incapable of substituting a measure to accompany their barbarous alterations.

One of the problems with free verse—which I commit occasionally—is that it is damned hard to remember—as even Gary Snyder acknowledges. Memorization, I believe, should go hand in hand with the reading and learning of poems. We can remember short verses like "In a Station of the Metro" and "The Red Wheel Barrow," but a long poem in free verse is virtually impossible to recite accurately. Lacking the chains of epithets which Homer used, all we have to help us is meter and rhyme.

ON A LINE FROM VALÉRY

ON A LINE FROM VALÉRY

Tout le ciel vert ce meurt. Le dernier arbre brule.

The whole green sky is dying. The last tree flares
With a great burst of supernatural rose
Under a canopy of poisonous airs.

Could we imagine our return to prayers
To end in time before time's final throes,
The green sky dying as the last tree flares?

But we were young in judgement, old in years
Who could make peace; but it was war we chose,
To spread its canopy of poisoning airs.

Not all our children's pleas or women's fears
Could save us from this hell. And now, God knows
His whole green sky is dying as it flares.

Our crops of wheat have turned to fields of tares.
This dreadful century staggers to its close
As the sky dies for us, its poisoned heirs.

All rain was dust. Its granules were our tears.
Throats burst as universal winter rose
To kill the whole green sky, the last tree bare
Beneath its canopy of poisoned air.

TWO SECTIONS FROM "PRO FEMINA"

TWO

I take as my theme "the Independent Woman,"
Independent but maimed: observe the exigent neckties

Choking violet writers: the sad slacks of stipple-faced matrons;
Indigo intellectuals, crop-haired and callous-toed,
Cute spectacles, chewed cuticles, aced out by full-time beauties
In the race for a male. Retreating to drabness, bad manners
And sleeping with manuscripts. Forgive our transgressions
of old gallantries as we hitch in chairs, light our own cigarettes,
Not expecting your care, having forfeited it by trying to get even.

But we need dependency, cosseting and well-treatment.
So do men sometimes. Why don't they admit it?
We will be cows for a while, because babies howl for us,
Be kittens or bitches, who want to eat grass now and then
For the sake of our health. But the role of pastoral heroine
Is not permanent, Jack. We want to get back to the meeting.

Knitting booties and brows, tartars or termagants, ancient
Fertility symbols, chained to our cycle, released
Only in part by devices of hygiene and personal daintiness,
Strapped into our girdles, held down, yet uplifted by man's
Ingenious constructions, holding coiffures in a breeze,
Hobbled and swathed in whimsey, tripping on feminine
Shoes with fool heels, losing our lipsticks, you, me,
In ephemeral stockings, clutching our handbags and packages.

Our masks, always in peril of smearing or cracking,
in need of continuous check in the mirror or silverware,
Keep us in thrall to ourselves, concerned with our surfaces.
Look at man's uniform drabness, his impersonal envelope!
Over chicken wrists or meek shoulders, a formal, hard-fibered
    assurance.
The drape of the male is designed to achieve self-forgetfulness.

So, Sister, forget yourself a few times and see where it gets you:
Up the creek, alone with your talent, sans everything else.
You can wait for the menopause, and catch up on your reading.
So primp, preen, prink, pluck and prize your flesh,
All posturings! All ravishment! All sensiblitiy!
Meanwhile, have you used your mind today?

What pomegranate raised you frrom the dead,
Springing, full-grown, from your own head, Athena?

THREE

I will speak about women of letters, for I'm in the racket.
Our biggest successes to date? Old maids to a woman.
And our saddest conspicuous failures? The married spinsters
On loan to the husbands they treated like surrogate fathers.
Think of that crew of self-pitiers, not-very-distant,
Who carried the torch for themselves and got first-degree burns.
Or the sad sonneteers, toast-and-teasdales we loved at thirteen;
Middle-aged virgins seducing the puerile anthologists
Through lust-of-the-mind; barbiturate-drenched Camilles
With continuous periods, murmuring softly on sofas
When poetry wasn't a craft but a sickly effluvium,
The air thick with incense, musk, and emotional blackmail.

I suppose they reacted from an earlier womanly modesty
When too many girls were scabs to their stricken sisterhood,
Impugning our sex to stay in good with the men,
Commencing their insecure bluster. How they must have
    swaggered
When women themselves endorsed their own inferiority!
Vestals, vassals and vessels, rolled into several,
They took notes in rolling syllabics, in careful journals,
Aiming to please a posterity that despises them.
But we'll always have traitors who swear that a woman
    surrenders
Her Supreme Function, by equating Art with aggression
And failure with Femininity. Still, it's just as unfair
To equate Art with Femininity, like a prettily-packaged
    commodity

When we are the custodians of the world's best-kept secret:
Merely the private lives of one-half of humanity.

But even with masculine dominance, we mares and mistresses
Produced some sleek saboteuses, making their cracks
Which the porridge-brained males of the day were too thick
   to perceive,
Mistaking young hornets for perfectly harmless bumblebees.
Being thought innocuous rouses some women to frenzy;
They try to be ugly by aping the ways of the men
And succeed. Swearing, sucking cigars and scorching the
   bedspread,

Slopping straight shots, eyes blotted, vanity-blown
In the expectation of glory: *she writes like a man!*
This drives other women mad in a mist of chiffon.
(One poetess draped her gauze over red flannels, a practical
   feminist.)

But we're emerging from all that, more or less,
Except for some lady-like laggards and Quarterly priestesses
Who flog men for fun, and kick women to maim competition.
Now, if we struggle abnormally, we may almost seem normal;
If we submerge our self-pity in disciplined industry;
If we stand up and be hated, and swear not to sleep with editors;
If we regard ourselves formally, respecting our true limitations
Without making an unseemly show of trying to unfreeze our
   assets;
Keeping our heads and our pride while remaining unmarried;
And if wedded, kill guilt in its tracks when we stack up the dishes
And defect to the typewriter. And if mothers, believe in the luck
   of our children,
Whom we forbid to devour us, whom we shall not devour,
And the luck of our husbands and lovers, who keep free women.

A MUSE OF WATER

We who must act as handmaidens
To our own goddess, turn too fast,

Trip on our hems, to glimpse the muse
Gliding below her lake or sea,
Are left, long-staring after her,
Narcissists by necessity;

Or water-carriers of our young
Till waters burst, and white streams flow
Artesian, from the lifted breast:
Cup-bearers then, to tiny gods,
Imperious table-pounders, who
Are final arbiters of thirst.

Fasten the blouse, and mount the steps
From kitchen taps to Royal Barge,
Assume the trident, don the crown,
Command the Water Music now
That men bestow on Virgin Queens;
Or, goddessing above the waist,

Appear as swan on Thames or Charles
Where iridescent foam conceals
The paddle-stroke beneath the glide:
Immortal feathers preened in poems!
Not our true, intimate nature, stained
by labor, and the casual tide.

Masters of civilization, you
Who moved to river bank from cave,
Putting up tents, and deities,
Though every rivulet wander through
The final, unpolluted glades
To cinder-bank and culvert-lip,

And all the pretty chatterers
Still round the pebbles as they pass
Lightly over their watercourse,
and even the calm rivers flow,

We have, while springs and skies renew,
Dry wells, dead seas, and lingering drouth.

Water itself is not enough.
Harness her turbulence to work
For man: fill his reflecting pools.
Drained for his cofferdams, or stored
In reservoirs for his personal use:
Turn switches! Let the fountains play!

And yet these buccaneers still kneel
Trembling at the water's verge:
"Cool River-Goddess, sweet ravine,
Spirit of pool and shade, inspire!"
So he needs poultice for his flesh.
So he needs water for his fire.

We rose in mists and died in clouds
Or sank below the trammeled soil
To silent conduits underground,
Joining the blind-fish, and the mole.
A gleam of silver in the shale:
Lost murmur! Subterranean moan!

So flows in dark caves, dries away,
What would have brimmed from bank to bank,
Kissing the fields you turned to stone,
Under the boughs your axes broke.
And you blame streams for thinning out,
Plundered by man's insatiate want?

Rejoice when a faint music rises
Out of a brackish clump of weeds,
Out of the marsh at ocean-side,
Out of the oil-stained river's gleam,
By the long causeways and gray piers
your civilizing lusts have made.

Discover the deserted beach
Where ghosts of curlews safely wade:
Here the warm shallows lave your feet
Like tawny hair of magdalens.
Here, if you care, and lie full-length,
Is water deep enough to drown.

PHYLLIS KOESTENBAUM
WRITING CRIMINALLY

I began writing sonnets when a private student suggested to me that, since I'd assigned her a sonnet, I might try writing one. I wrote more than 400 before I finished writing and revising them, ten years later. Life and art were shaky, and sonnet writing became a way of surviving. Form created an apparent music. It also restrained the emotional intensity of my subject matter: crime, including the holocaust. I didn't write in a strict meter. I chose a more or less ten-syllable line (as close to ten as worked). I used a rhyme scheme, but the rhymes were only rarely exact, and, frankly, often didn't please me. I decided I was writing criminally: this notion did please me. Writing sonnets became an obsession, but the bigger obsession came with the revision process, which took as long as the writing. While I was writing sonnets, I wrote sestinas, villanelles, and other forms, but the sonnet, as a brief, habitual transcription of a life out of control, and controlled, became the controlling form.

SONNET XXXVII FROM "CRIMINAL SONNETS"

I'd decided I initiate most
sex and held back, feeling no more or less
sexual than usual; the morning post—
no sex I feel, as usual, anxious,
wondering if I'd begun would he have
continued and was he with another
woman earlier. In Iran's Evin

Prison small children must watch their mothers
tortured; in Soviet penal institutions
dissidents are given pain-inducing
drugs; there are 98 inhuman nations—
castrations, burnings, amputations: endured;
not. I can't go faster, must get through this
work I fault myself for: too many sonnets.

SYBIL KOLLAR
CALISTHENICS

The architecture of the poem in relation to content always holds a mystery. Reading Dickinson, I decided to enter the dynasty of formalism—slowly, in steps. At first, it was the sheer calisthenics that was appealing; I had become an acrobat. I bounded about within a fixed arena until gradually the forms became more natural. Later, a series of sonnets on family secrets emerged. The nature of the secret is to discourage disclosure, and the sonnet provides a boundary within which the telling of the secret is kept safe. The form also offers a counterbalance for the expression of emotion in which the forbidden is revealed. "Sunday Matinee" and "Late Arrivals" are in this series.

SUNDAY MATINEE

At the movies i always love the look
of food on the plates, mysterious mounds
being eaten by cowhands, kitchen nooks
with steaming pots, knives clicking, sucking sounds.
My father puts popcorn in my small hands
as a lady with dark lipstick rushes
toward the skinny cowboy smoking while he stands
leering at her. They meet. His mouth brushes
her cheek. A man's coat covers my right knee
as a posse thunders away. A thin finger

moves up my thigh. My father will not hear
my whispered plea. He shifts his weight, lingers.
Finally, he appeases his petulant child—
we exchange seats while outlaws camp in the wild.

LATE ARRIVALS

At forty-six I am still the baby
of the family. Born ten years after
my sister, I am a joke, a maybe,
a whim. Passover, my parent's laughter
drifts across the table as Rafe arrives
late. Their life-long friend and I share little.
Yet his gifts of bears lined my shelves at five,
his silly stories always held a riddle
I never guessed. My mother's fingers skip
up his dark sleeve like dancers. Their eyes lift.
I see my face and hair as his, our lips
full on the bottom. Their locked gaze shifts
and for a moment they are watching me
as if wondering what I've come to see.

MAXINE KUMIN
Paradoxical Freedom

The joy of working in form is, for me, the paradoxical freedom form bestows to say the hard truths. Constraints of rhyme and/or meter liberate the poet to confront difficult or painful or elegiac material, often elevating the language to heights unattainable in free verse, to say nothing of the extra music form admits.

THE HEIGHT OF THE SEASON

Once a time is how the baby asks for a story
wandering from person to person patiently seeking
a teller of Three Bears or Riding Hood to take him in.
Clutching the book he pleads with his nine-year-old
    cousin
Once a time? Have it? meaning to solve the mystery
of words he has come to love but cannot unlock.

Once when my father's heart was starting to stop
I took him blackberry jam and we sat in his cubicle
in the Pennsylvania Graduate Hospital
spreading its sugar on saltines, not so much
a study in contrasts as a way safely to touch.
I was glad that my father had died, his optimism
intact, the year before Jack Kennedy was shot
and Jackie sat wiping his blood and brains from her
    suit.
Glad that my father was spared that televised vision.

In *once a time* a different language is spoken.
The landscape is sweet there, free of briar or bracken.

The animals talk in reasonable tones that children
can understand. As tonight at the stove three women
converse over berries, mashing the afternoon's
   pickings
with sugar in the pot. This is the height of the season,
ripeness enfolds us. My daughters and I remember
the absent enthusiast, the goddess, my mother
who sieved seeds from gallons of pulp with a fervor
we cannot match, though we long to extend the
   continuum.

Meanwhile at the kitchen table a game begins
with dice and six counters and a book of questions.
The categories are constant: always Sports,
Geography, Current Events, History and the Arts
(largely cinema stars the vintage of Liz Taylor),
a game the nine-year-old is intent on winning
while the baby wanders from player to player
   inquiring
have it? and wax is melted to seal the jars.
A benevolent rain swells tomorrow's cucumbers
and reddening tomatoes (what else must I save?)
as the axis turns, spilling us into fall
until, in tears now with his *have it?*
the tired baby will have it all.

THE NUNS OF CHILDHOOD:
TWO VIEWS

O where are they now, your harridan nuns
who thumped on young heads with a metal thimble
and punished with rulers your upturned palms:

three smacks for failing in long division,
one more to instill the meaning of *humble.*
As the twig is bent, said your harridan nuns.

Once, a visiting bishop, serene
at the close of a Mass through which he had shambled,
smiled upon you with upturned palms.

"Because this is my feast day," he ended,
"you may all have a free afternoon." In the scramble
of whistles and cheers one harridan nun,

fiercest of all the parochial coven,
Sister Pascala, without preamble
raged, "I protest!" and rapping on palms

at random, had bodily to be restrained.
O God's perfect servant is kneeling on brambles
wherever they sent her, your harridan nun,
enthroned as a symbol with upturned palms.

2.

O where are they now, my darling nuns
whose heads were shaved under snowy wimples,
who rustled drily inside their gowns,

disciples of Oxydol, starch and bluing,
their backyard clothesline a pious example?
They have flapped out of sight, my darling nuns.

Seamless as fish, made all of one skin,
their language secret, these gentle vestals
were wedded to Christ inside their gowns.

O Mother Superior Rosarine
on whose lap the privileged visitor lolled
—I at age four with my darling nuns,

with Sister Elizabeth, Sister Ann,
am offered to Jesus, the Jewish child-
next-door, who worships your ample black gown.

your eyebrows, those thick mustachioed twins,
your rimless glasses, your ring of pale gold—
who can have stolen my darling nuns?
Who rustles drily inside my gown?

DESPAIR

is a mildewed tent. Under the center pole
you must either bend double or take to your knees.
And suppose, after all that tugging and smoothing, you ease
yourself, blind end first, into your blanket roll—
wet under, and over, wool scratch, and you lying still,
lashed down for the season, hands crossed between your thighs,
the canvas stink in your nose, the night in your eyes—
what makes you think that rattling your ribs here will
save you? Camper, you are a bone-sore fool.
Somewhere a brown moth beats at a lighted window.
Somewhere a weasel fastens into his mouse.
The ground heaves up its secret murmur of toadstools;
they are marching to bear you away to the dumb show.
Yank up the pegs and come back! Come back in the house.

PHILLIS LEVIN
Embracing Fate

When I entered my freshman year of college I showed an alarmingly large manuscript of poems to one of the poets offering a workshop that semester. He weighed the manuscript in his hands, and then began to browse through page after page, skipping around and quoting lines he found especially felicitous or clumsy. He seemed to be looking for something in particular that he could not find. After a pause he asked me to show him a poem written in the first person that was not in rhyme and meter. Until that moment it had not occurred to me that since the age of twelve I had been writing with an unconscious system. I wrote many poems in free verse, and many more in blank verse or deploying both rhyme and meter, but most of my work in free verse was in the third person, and everything in the first person was in meter. So there was nothing—not one poem—I could show him that was free of measure and also in the first person.

The polarization of first person poems in measure and third person poems in free verse (some in rhyme and meter) was not a conscious choice. I needed to speak in the first person from a more formalized space, perhaps to give myself the distance necessary to overcome my introversion. Perhaps I needed—and continue to need—formal elements in order to create a ritualized experience that would allow me to exist in the bounds of the poem (a field of play) instead of the bounds of life, to enter an altered state, a heightened relation to the temporal. It was embarrassing to the other students that I didn't know I wasn't supposed to be doing this. How had I managed to avoid entering the modern world—that is, the mid-seventies—when it was especially out of fashion to read anything that wasn't contemporary or to write in a style alluding in any way to the subjects and forms of a literary tradition, i.e., to write under the influence of anything other than one's own immediate personal history? It had never occurred to me that I had to make a choice, yet somehow I was beginning to feel pressured, as if there were an allegiance I had failed to make and a loyalty I should have separated myself from.

Not until I was twenty-five did I allow myself to return to experimenting with meter, off-rhyme and rhyme. This change was precipitated by a conversation with a British critic who had read my poems and remarked on their internal music, and how he felt that I was resisting my own musicality, not allowing it to develop. Yes, I had internalized the subtle censorship of the 1970's, and now I had to return to the source and learn how to write the poems my ear wanted to hear while making a sense that was not obscure and hermetic, as was my earliest work. Writing almost exclusively in free verse for five years had separated me from what had come too easily, and thus when I began to work again with meter and rhyme my poems showed a confluence of more forces and possibilities, a familiarity with the contemporary idiom combined with a greater understanding of texture and prosody.

For me embracing form is a form of embracing fate, of simultaneously accepting and resisting, absorbing and shaping the forces of language and life, the interplay of the arbitrary and the given with the shaped and the chosen. So if, for example, my poem "Dark

Horse" is halting in cadence, fluid and then awkward, one will feel and hear and see the meaning that is not stated, one will be involved through the prosody in my portrait of this horse, who embodied beauty, mystery, form, delicacy, vulnerability, and nobility. It is not necessary to know that I was thinking of Poland when writing this poem, that I had befriended a Polish painter who had spent hours talking of his country's complex history, and its tragic position in 1984 before the fall of Communism; that I had seen this horse before and after this conversation, and that the horse began to embody a country, whose fate was that of a dark horse. But I felt I had to create in the poem an internal music that would be a simulacrum of the heavy and light, the gentle and the harsh, the fast and the slow. I searched for patterns of sound that would suggest the intrinsic relationship of the auditory and the visual, that would transform the coincidences of sound into an inevitable, evocative meaning. In the last line of the fourth stanza, "Dry leaves sighing through wind and tears," I attempted to bind these correspondences as tightly as possible in order to create a synesthetic effect. And so the word "sighing" carries in it the long "i" and the long "e" that occur first in the word "dry," then in the word "leaves," vowels that recur as echoes in "wind" and "tears." There are other presences at work here, as well, including an allusion to Auden's "The Fall of Rome" and Hardy's "During Wind and Rain," two poems that opened the possibility of intensifying both density and clarity. Perhaps my relationship to form and rhythm is a constant struggle to come as close as possible to the impossible. I suppose I am looking for wholeness and completion, or at least the patterns that call into being an image of wholeness and completion.

CITIZENS & SKY

The city branching blindly through the clouds,
Its stream of walls, its flame of flashing glass,
Its buildings without wonder, windowless.
Aghast, the heartbeat booming underground.

There's something in the air: a currency
Whose random courses sweep us into crowds.
Beyond the fog our trees are grazing in,
Glitter gulls on errands from the sea.

Just now a jet broke through, clearing over
This geometric wave, these figures, bent
On getting home, colliding in blossoms
Without design, dissolving into sound.

DARK HORSE
(for Włodzimierz Ksiazek)

Like a child's cut-out, she holds her weight
Against the stiff, encroaching cold,
Standing so none may pass without
Gleaning the gravity of her load.

The wooden fence warps slightly; flakes
Cleave where shadows fall; her black skin,
Dense as winter silence, invokes
The long interval before she'll turn.

Resounding signs of sudden thaw
In rising tones of dripping snow
Compose deep caverns enclosing dawn,
Uncoiling secrets vast and slow.

Come walk inside this blinding space
And know it is made of ears and eyes
Compounding years of clouds and ice,
Dry leaves sighing through wind and tears.

Then if the centuries seem too sad,
The world withholding its love and shame,
Study this dark horse in a field
Who bows her head to time.

PLANTING ROSES

Digging deep in the garden
My father hit a buried hive,
A thousand thorns rose around him:
"Run into the house," he cried.

I ran away but he stayed,
Taking the stings so I could flee;
Darkening waves of angry blind
Bees repeated, "Where is she?"

All that night inside a dream
I kept my father from his pain
And sang to him among the bees:
"O father, do not save me."

JANET LEWIS
A KIND OF CELEBRATION

In the beginning poetry can be a kind of celebration that calls for a certain formality and enhancement of emotion. It is not a prose statement. And as a creation it demands music of its own, or in itself. Just as there are dance forms the body is happy in, I think there are forms, such as the sonnet, the villanelle, and the other stanza forms, in which the language is happy. And the mind is happy to find these forms in language. They are artificial like dancing but they do something for the emotions, for it gives us pleasure to move in these forms.

I was schooled in the stanza forms of English verse both at school and by my father, and learned the different types of stanzas and metrical lines available in the tradition. As the years passed I wrote a great many songs—not necessarily to be set to music but to exist in a lyrical form. Later work borders on essay but stays very loosely within a metrical form. Besides this, I write reams of prose and am careful that it should not be poetry.

Although prose is itself, I think, rhythmical, generally in verse the rhythmical units are shorter. But there is in verse a metrical beat under the rhythm. Rhythm and meter go together, supporting one another, yet rhythmical units of verse run counter to the metrical as much as they run with it. And that's what makes it interesting. The rhythm and meter comment on each other. We need meter. Otherwise, we fall into prose.

TIME AND MUSIC

"Here. Trapped in Time."—Y.W.

Time, that gives to music life,
Measuring the motion's strife,
Time, the substance and the breath,
For melody is Time the death.

The melody upon it rides
Like fisher's boat upon the tides,
Or like the swallow through the air—
And vanishes while flying there.

And we, like music, through it move,
Or, lost from it, unqualitied,
From life as well as death are freed
And no design nor beauty prove.

"Here, trapped in Time," but Time for us
Both snare and breath and motion is.

154

VASSAR MILLER
A WORTHWHILE TASK

I use form often. When I'm writing a sonnet, I have trouble making the language sound natural, but I enjoy the challenge. It's like doing any other worthwhile task. It's the challenge of doing something difficult well.

LIGHT READING

Spies whisper through my air condition units.
My drainpipes crawl with wraiths of Jack the Ripper.
A time bomb in my oven ticks off minutes,
Imperiling beans and porkchops for my dinner.
An ex-con feeds my watchdogs poisoned candy
And saws my burglar bars in half. My lodgers
Are little men from Mars named Rick and Randy
Cloned from the brave Flash Gordon and Buck
    Rogers.
Bats breed inside my breakfast room and kitchen,
Where paranoid pygmies plot their crimes.
My hundred-watt bulbs are hung with lichen.
A ghost squats on my toilet. Between times,
If things grow dull, old Nazi bombers strafe.
So, ringed with ghouls and corpses, I am safe.

HOW FAR?

How far is it to you by foot?
Ten thousand stones,
Two million grains of dust and soot,
All my bruised bones.

How far is it to you by sea?
Twelve hills and hollows
Of water, each one risking me
Gulped in salt swallows.

How far is it to you by rail?
A myriad meadows
Sweeping the window in a gale
Of golden shadows.

How far is it to you by air?
Ten thousand thunders,
Countless ice crystals set aflare
With rainbow wonders.

How far is it to you by light?
Two parted petals
Of eyelids flowering with sight
Where sunshine settles.

How far is it to you by love?
I have no notion.
For so to seek and find you prove
One selfsame motion.

DIRGE IN JAZZ TIME
(for Sophie Tucker)

Her voice forever match to dry wood
Since, a girl, she sang for a crust,
Her innocence even then understood
As a subtler word for lust
As in age her wisdom would mean delight—
Red-hot Mama who is cold tonight.

Her voice in the veins of every man
Like radiant fire would glisten

Till his body, tuned ear, did nothing else than
Keep cocked to her tones and listen.
But the lilt in his bones has taken flight,
Since Red-hot Mama is cold tonight.

"One of these days you'll miss me." Oh yes,
Though they couldn't credit it then
That she who had flashed in the sequined dress
And danced in the nerves of men
Should have given them this terrible slight,
Not Red-hot Mama grown cold tonight!

Turn the spotlight off of the night-club floor.
Let the jazzmen muffle their drums
And their saxophones she will hear no more
Where winter forever numbs,
Where no one can warm her whose heart burned bright,
Where Red-hot Mama is cold tonight.

LESLIE MONSOUR
Notes on Contemporary Formalism

In 1984, when I began seriously to consider a career as a poet, nearly everyone I encountered was writing in free verse. Rhyme was tolerated if it was haphazard or accidental. Meter was unheard of. In workshops, poets alluded to the rhythm of poetry but were never specific, except to say that it was different from the rhythm of prose. These workshops were like music classes where no one knew how to read music; we listened as we each hummed our tunes, and we talked about the way they sounded, and the way they made us feel. But we skipped the basic, important questions of key signature and beats per measure. Most of the poets I knew seemed to be under the impression that writing in meter or using a regular rhyme scheme was unprofessional. No one wanted to do it. These poets were overlooking some of the most elemental poetic tools the language has to offer. They were ignoring the roots of our linguistic history and forgetting that meter makes language memorable. I didn't know this at the time. But I did know that many of my poems seemed unfinished to me. I wasn't satisfied with their "open" forms. I began to find the landscape of free verse impoverished and monotonous in its unhorizoned vastness, its imperious limitlessness and its vague, indistinct shapes.

After Timothy Steele arrived in Los Angeles, I took two of his classes at U.C.L.A. In 1987 he taught "Writing in Meter," and, in 1988, "The Short Poem," using a rational, mathematical, and gratifyingly athletic approach to the craft of poetry. He refreshed our dim recollections of the traditional stress patterns and taught us effective and suitable variations and substitutions, the effects of rising and falling line endings and weak and strong enjambments, and how to be fluent within metric constrictions. Working on poems this way felt vital and healthy. It was like going back to visit the farm. There was nothing vague about it. Instead of rambling through a rocky field, scattering seeds at random, we paced off our parcels, stood behind the plough and team, took up hoes, spades and trowels, and planted evenly-spaced seeds in regular, cultivated rows, arriving at far better results. Tim Steele had the patience, dedication and guts of a Peace Corps volunteer.

I've found that I am a great fan of symmetry. I always have been. Symmetry is a natural phenomenon of life. It is not artificial. As a child, I loved to peer into both ends of a kaleidoscope and observe how one end was just the trapped bits of colored glass lying in a heap. Up through the opposite end, I could see where the mirrors cut through the circle, reflecting and organizing the shapes into equal parts of color and light, transforming the formless mass into a symmetrical design of breathtaking beauty. (The most carefully made kaleidoscopes have the least noticeable mirrors. It's the crudely made ones that diminish the effect by using thick, uneven, cheap reflectors. The same is true of poetic devices). Of course, in applying symmetry to poetic expression, the real trick is to come up with a design that also achieves clarity of meaning. It is my conclusion that formalist poets make a more conscious effort to be understood than their informal counterparts.

Robert Frost observed that real poetry is experienced by responding to "meaning struck across the rigidity of meter.... Form is true to the conflict of law and liberty.... To claim exemption, to demand unfettered expression, is to insist on staying at bat after one has swung three times." How appropriate to relate poetry to baseball, the sport with the most beautifully designed symmetry of all. Since I am a woman, the world of professional baseball is open to me only as a spectator. This is not true of poetry. If I choose to step up to the plate as a formalist, it is not to condemn free verse. Powerful poems have been written in that medium, and I may yet write poems that work successfully in the old experiment. But I know that if I ever acquire the skill and grace to hit a poetic home run, it can only happen if I stand behind the line and count my swings, not reducing my achievement, but elevating it to the formal standards of the game's history.

EMILY'S WORDS

Unsquandered, sure and quiet as a root,
She stayed at home all dressed in pleated white,
And accurately weighed the brain of God,
The sum of acts not carried out. Unwed,
That she not be divided, she stayed whole,
And heard the sound the tooth makes in the soul.
A little knife that cuts through at a slant,
Her voice, a child's, ungendered, wasn't meant
For "Our Fathers" murmured under Sunday trees,
But rang like axe strokes on the frozen seas.
"Called back," she wrote, the mourners treading so,
That from her gypsy face a light broke through.
She died in May, and one thing struck them all:
The coffin was astonishingly small.

SWEEPING

I whisk the litter from my mother's tomb.
I do it blind, I do it in my sleep—
While dreaming to the rhythm of the broom,

The ancient, tidal motion of her womb.
I'm very good at shoring up a heap—
It quiets all the corners of the room,

Where prayers have shed the echo of their weep:
The patterns on the rug begin to bloom,
And muted shadows sing as they grow deep;

I hear the bristles breathing when I sweep.

A DREAM OF DYING

The hammock was a blue cocoon,
And I, its seeing worm,
A fading tune, a crescent moon,
The threads about me, firm.

I fell into a purr of sleep
Amid the greeny glint,
The dewy weep, the leafy sweep
Of myrtle and of mint.

And while I slept, the tree went round
In galaxies of shade,
Till every pound and every sound
Were blissfully unmade,

And I was scattered everywhere,
As nothing in no place;
No web of air, no net of care,
No earth, no tree, no face.

HONOR MOORE
THE WALLS OF THE ROOM

I wasn't going to be incarcerated in "their" forms, was how I saw it in 1970. I was infused with the energies of feminism—we were inventing a new poetry. Yet, as I became more experienced, I became frustrated. While responding to a sheaf of poems I had brought to him, a poet suggested syllabics, sent me to read Auden and Marianne Moore. I was skeptical: I wrote a more "confessional" poetry than either of them. Direct emotion was an element of my integrity as a poet. But I was intrigued. I began to count syllables. I made my own rules, which were in the direction of condensation and difficulty. I found I relished technical challenge. I began to play with the counterpoint of syllabic sequence and sentence, to see enjambment as an opportunity to encode a poem with messages which would deepen or set off its ostensible "story." After a while, syllabics became my instrument.

Then I was seduced, in readings I heard Marilyn Hacker give, by the sestina. The incantatory dramatics of the recurring end-words haunted and challenged me. Having created my own forms, was it possible to appropriate one of "theirs"? I attempted several sestinas, enough to be daunted. I was not ready.

I had some material which had been lying around in notebooks for a few years. I had read about the murder trial of Joanne Little. A black woman in the South had stabbed with an ice pick a prison guard who was raping her. The prosecutor was quoted as saying, "What!? You didn't holler, you didn't shout, you didn't fight him off?" When I thought of the absurdity of the question, seeing in my mind the small black woman and her looming, beefy attacker, I remembered an incident from my childhood. I had written some lines about Joanne Little's experience. Now I began to write my own memories: a small room at dusk, my baby brother, the young male baby sitter dressed in black, hair slicked like Elvis Presley. But what I had written would not cohere, and I put it aside.

A couple of winters later, I went to the MacDowell Colony. One morning, as I walked the narrow snow-packed road through the forest to my studio, I heard the rumble behind me of a car and stepped aside, barely in time, as a man, a fellow colonist, swerved toward me in a gas guzzling American sedan, a leering grin on his red, bulbous face. I reached my studio, sat down at my desk, and, still shaking with fear, pulled out the material about the babysitter dressed in black. When the car lurched toward me on the snowy path, I had become the young woman facing her attacker, myself at five years old, powerless to protect myself.

I began to write, raw in my childhood memory, and the poem came, taking dramatic, sequential shape in the sestina form. Its restraint became the walls of the room, the recurrence of end words a verbal equivalent for the relentlessness of the molester's intentions. Embraced in its sure architecture, the violated child, silenced for thirty years, is free to tell her story.

FIRST TIME: 1950

In the back bedrrom, laughing when you pull
something fawn-colored from your black
tight pants, the unzipped chino slit.
I keep myself looking at the big belt
buckled right at my eyes, feel the hand
riffle my hair: You are called Mouse, baby-

sitter trusted Wednesdays with my baby
brother. With me. I still see you pull
that huge bunch of keys from a pocket, hand
them to my brother, hear squeaking out back—
Mrs. Fitz's clothesline—as you unbelt,
turn me to you, my face to the open slit.

It's your skin, this thing, head, its tiny slit
like the closed eye of a still-forming baby.
As you stroke, it stiffens like a new belt—
your face gets almost sick. I want to pull
away, but you grip my arm. I see by your black
eyes you won't let go. With your left hand

you take my chin. With your other hand
you guide it, head reddening, into my slit,
my five-year-old mouth. In the tight black
quiet of my shut eyes, I hear my baby
brother shaking the keys. You lurch, pull
at my hair. I don't breathe, feel buckle, belt,

pant. It tastes lemony, musty as a belt
after a day of sweat. Mouth hurts, my hands
push at your hips. I gag. You let me pull
free. I open my eyes, see the strange slits
yours are; you don't look at me. "Babe, babee—"
You are moaning, almost crying. The black

makes your skin clam-white now, your jewel-black
eyes blacker. You buckle up the thick belt.
When you take back the keys, my baby
brother cries. You extend a shaking hand
you make kind. In daylight through a wide slit
an open shade leaves, I see her pull,

Mrs. Fitz pulling in her rusty, soot-black
line. Framed by a slit, her window, her large hands
flash, sort belts, dresses, shirts, baby clothes.

A GREEN PLACE

"What's beyond making love?" A true question.
"Time," I quip, knowing my imagining
seeks an answer to soothe fear from your face. If
we could freeze the instant in sex when light
shudders and we let time go, the clear
light of morning which turns lush green

silvery. Beyond making love? Green
if it's a place. Here any question
leads to an answer if put clearly,
here all responsive gestures feed imagining
and nature has no difficulty. Light
of noon: We are making love as if

it is a path. I am kissing you as if
what I drink from you is a river through green
breath, as if you are a source of light,
as if the feel of your mouth rendered questions
obsolete, as if simple imagining
extended vision without exacting a clear

equivalent in risk. Beyond this? Clear
dark of evening shadows your face. If
we lived as though time were, like imagining,
an easy skittering, an ascent through green
familiarity till colors, like questions,
need no assured compliment, then light,

freed of its debt to time, could make light
of fear, leave just what grief makes clear—
smooth pebbles in a crystal bowl. But questions
like yours darken like night or storm. What if
I can't answer? I see you in a green
place looking at me, but my imagining

doesn't speak in answers. Imagining
is formed in a slow rush of memory: light,
fear, sound, weather. Ecstatic smell of new green,
touch of a lover's skin, cheek, mouth. Clear
liquid glinting in sunlight dazzle. If
you insist I answer, the question

is lost to your imagining. If I claim clear
knowledge, light that loosens memory darkens. If
love's beyond love, it's green. We share the question.

SUZANNE NOGUERE
A Living Thing

When I was fifteen my older brother, Philip, introduced me to modern poetry. It was a passion of his and immediately became a passion of mine. Philip loved Hart Crane in particular and wrote his own virtuoso poems of almost dizzying invention and scintillation as well as spare free verse poems. I wrote free verse, villanelles, rondeaus, and quatrains. We were both intoxicated with language and with rhetoric. It was an unanticipated event of adolescence: suddenly the mind too was different.

Since then, having started with the moderns, I have read backward in time, always finding iambic pentameter and tetrameter lines that stick in the mind as if each had its own receptor site: the cell membrane opens, the words enter.

And the words stay. If my thoughts could be read in digital display like the latest news circling the tower in Times Square, they would flash with lines first read all those years ago—"They came like swallows and like swallows went"—"Especially when the October wind"—and with all the poems of Hopkins, those that are regular in form and those that show that both line and form are not static but can expand, contract, and mutate like a living thing.

THE SCRIBES

THESCRIBESPACKEDCAPITALSACROSSTHEPAGE
as if they were still chiseling stone until
at last in minuscules they fixed a wedge
of space between the words and a hush fell
upon the page as if light filtered through
trees to a forest floor. It is the space
inside the vessel, said Lao-tzu,
that is its usefulness. It is the space
inside the u that gives it life. And where
the leaflets of the white ash meet the stalk,
not sessile but set a space apart, the air
moves in between them in the give and take
of interpenetration, as nearing
the end, the poem itself comes to a clearing.

THE SECRET

Nathaniel, born Hathorne, you who set
the scarlet letter A on Hester's bosom
as the world's avenging epithet
to scorch the roots where it had found the blossom,
what secret was there in your own heart when
you slipped the W into your name?
Some Wilderness you would not yield, a green
reserve where in their privacy thoughts came?
Or was it Wonder always at your core?
Or Witch or Woman, Will, or Word to mark
the curse upon your name in Salem lore
and at the same time sever from that dark
inheritance? Or deeper than a double
meaning, was there a double you akin
to the small thorned tree whose branches are
     brambles
where a songbird is safe? Was there a twin

heart in the heartwood forming slowly, tough
as oak, that paced your twelve-year solitude?
Was hardiness in poor soil a proof
of possibility? Or thorns amid
the whitest flowers in spring the truth in view?
The berries?—scarlet in winter! Now, small tree,
if there be any empathy in you,
take to yourself that last emphatic E.

WHIRLING ROUND THE SUN

Sometimes it seems almost beyond belief
to be here whirling round the sun: this view
of buildings taller than trees, trees, and the blue
sky unmoved like a truth graphed on the chief
coordinates of my window frame. Yet leaf
by leaf turning gives my slow mind a clue
to earth's revolution and with such hue
sometimes it seems almost beyond belief
to see. As a bus speeds me through the park
past maple, sourgum, and sweetgum's clearer
color, so fast along my nerves the sparks
fly to my brain with their electric sign
for scarlet, then make my mind a mirror
of amber; and the effort is not mine.

SOMA

This body deemed machine—not daemon flesh
that makes itself from a given seed and springs
up in a reptile's egg with the bones of a fish,
from fins makes fingers and flour telic limbs—
propels each cell into the fetal mesh
to feed and be fed by the heart, brain, and lungs.
But on the off chance that this might not be,
try Ockham's razor on that trinity.

My heart keeps up its obbligato to
my every thought, intrudes its presence as
I fall asleep feeling its to-and-fro,
so that it seems a mackerel swims in place
beneath my ribs, delaying death just so
long as it keeps on moving. Yet this ace
half pound of muscle never falters, fit
to function: matter with a mother wit.

My brain's empowered by that primal pluck
but almost could believe itself the critter
superior to all, for watch it shuck
off body with an avid thrust the better
to be the avatar proclaimed a book—
as if the body of one's work were fitter
with its glittering spine shining on the shelf
to house that essence of oneself, one's elf.

And all the while still the brain's high notion
of its own inspiration follows from
the sole exemplar of the lungs in motion.
Not housed; inherent; everything I am—
each grief, belief, and elemental passion—
starts and snaps with this living frame.
Account me compost when my lungs are through
and the true salt water of my blood turns blue.

Then colonies of me in their remote
substrata, cells that rallied with each omen,
will perish one by one and bring about
the dissolution of my soul, my soma.
Lying without a pulse or breath or thought,
my body steels itself in that long moment
before it festers, as it cools to ice.
It will not witness Halley's comet twice.

BARNEY BIGARD

Solo or in the ride out gliding and
soaring through three and a half octaves like
the swallow-tailed kite sure in air on land

and sea and seeming half on fire in quick
drops through the cypress swamp, its white and jet
feathers fanned like palmetto, making thick

gloom glorious, swooping as if to whet
the heart with startling grace, he makes the air
move, peerless and clear, in the clarinet.

In chalumeau it comes out, *la chaleur*
of New Orleans, in upper range the reck-
less runs he mastered in Chicago where,

when King Oliver asked him to go back
to the hard instrument the Tios taught,
he stood amidst the live and water oak

in spirit, bent his own will like a note,
and worked until all tones below the staff
were the dark blue of the great river's throat.

There are days when the mind amazes itself
with phrases and keen, melancholy breaks
that state the facts exactly, as if

the mind itself were heated like the wax
of an unpressed record, ready for the die
casting of indelible phrases as

his fingers spring from the fast keys, then fly
back into the black wood with a Creole cry.

ELISE PASCHEN
From the "Inside Out"

When I think about prosody, some words of Yeats's come to mind: "If I wrote of personal love or sorrow in free verse, or in any rhythm that left it unchanged, amid all its accidence, I would be full of self-contempt because of my egotism and indiscretion, and foresee the boredom of my reader. I must choose a traditional stanza, even what I alter must seem traditional...." Although Yeats overstates the case, his words illustrate an important aspect of his aesthetic. Yeats's love poems often originated from a deeply personal emotion. Yet by revising and by adopting a traditional stanza, he created an enduring work of art.

Seamus Heaney first made me aware of the importance of revision. I was fortunate to have had the chance to study poetry with him at college where, in trying to teach me the necessity of revision, he suggested I look at Yeats's manuscripts at Houghton Library, which allowed me to witness how extensively Yeats drafted and redrafted his poems.

The other ground-breaking experience I had at college was in Robert Fitzgerald's Versification course in which we studied the history of English prosody. We were asked to memorize short passages in different meters. Then we attempted to recreate through our own exercises each metrical form, from classical alcaics and sapphics, to Anglo-Saxon strong stress meter, to blank verse and, finally, free verse. Through our studies, we came to recognize the contrapuntal structure of a poem, how meter may be counterpointed by the living speech of the line.

I had written poems since I was a child and always had been instinctively drawn to poetry's music. But not until Fitzgerald's class did I learn about the musical properties of meter and how to measure a line of verse. Having been surrounded by classical music from an early age, I realized that scanning poetry and writing in meter were like learning and practicing scales on a piano. I practiced scales by writing poems from the "outside in." I would choose a form first, for example, a sonnet, sestina, quatrains, etc., and then stumble upon discoveries within formal perimeters. The form would occasion unaccustomed turns and fresh departures in the poem as it unfolded.

Although I still enjoy playing with traditional forms, I am intrigued by how form emerges from the process of organic composition. Poems, also, may be written from the "inside out." The first draft may happen quickly. I then try to recognize the poem's configuration, its meter or rhythm, and attempt to give the poem voice and shape. The following weeks or months are then devoted to revision! Or, to quote the title of this anthology and the opening lines of Emily Dickinson's poem: "After great pain, a formal feeling comes—"

LITANY

To light the dark
of you where no
light has explored,

to trek the deserts,
accept mirages,
swim gulfs, inhabit

the islands, caves,
the rooms and alcoves
of you, the chambers,

to chart the arteries,
to join the valves,
the bolts, the nails,

to open windows,
to hazard exits,
fall through trap floors,

to upend drawers,
slam doors, to shatter
the glass of you,

but most of all,
awake or sleeping,
to learn to say:

No more to you.

CONFEDERACY

Wear the heart like a home
as in Patsy Kline's song,
what we're two-stepping to,

my heart worn on his sleeve.
This is Nashville. I'm in
a spin, a stranger's arms.

Commandeering my moves,
he inquires, "Where's your home?"
I confuse "home" for "heart"

since revolving with him
is like sipping sloe gin,
and, because he's a soldier,

I'm inclined to consume
his Confederacy.
We ignore the dance floor's

grooves, whirl round, and then dip
while his fingers dig deep
in the trench of my spine.

But my heart is half-cocked
as it beats against his
regimentals, then stops.

His badge strikes my heart home.
On the edge of surrender
I open my heart

just to see if he'll scare:
I describe those gunmen
who keep aiming each night,

firing bullets my way,
miscellaneous shots,
which never hit their mark

but awake me, instead.
They're embedded, I say,
in my home, in my heart.

MOLLY PEACOCK
ONE GREEN, ONE BLUE:
ONE POINT ABOUT FORMAL VERSE WRITING
AND ANOTHER ABOUT WOMEN WRITING
FORMAL VERSE

The dazzling confusion of style and substance, like a brilliant feather one cannot say for sure is absolutely green or absolutely blue, is what we refer to when we say that form creates content in a poem and content form. But this forgets the initial palette of the creator of the poem, who knows (or hopes she knows) how much green and how much blue are required for the mix. Common wisdom says that the poet must choose the suitable form for the subject, where the mind and the language are at one. It says appropriateness is all: the form must be capable of the same gesture as the feeling. Supporting this is the brilliance of finished poems, their iridescence far removed from the initial palette the poet composed, where the blue was distinctly blue, the green distinctly green, and the leap of the imagination still.

I feel the initial choice, the conscious choice, of one traditional verse form over another, is not always the choice to match the feeling, but rather a choice to contain, to control, or otherwise make the feeling safe to explore. Take Elizabeth Bishop's late poem "Pink Dog" for example. Here are the first four stanzas, which occur during mardi gras:

PINK DOG
(Rio de Janeiro)

The sun is blazing and the sky is blue.
Umbrellas clothe the beach in every hue.
Naked, you trot across the avenue.

Oh, never have I seen a dog so bare!
Naked and pink, without a single hair...
Startled, the passersby draw back and stare.

Of course they're mortally afraid of rabies.
You are not mad; you have a case of scabies
but look intelligent. Where are your babies?

(A nursing mother, by those hanging teats.)
In what slum have you hidden them, poor bitch,
while you go begging, living by your wits?

Why on earth would she choose to use rhymed trip-
lets? What a bumpy, comic way in which to lavish solic-
itude on a hairless bitch out without her babies during
carnival in Rio. But the enormity of the subject for Bishop—
a mother dog who has abandoned her children to en-
ter the mad world of carnival just as Elizabeth Bishop's
own mother abandoned her and was consigned to a
mental institution—is not at all comic. The depth of
feeling does not match the form; it is much larger than
tercets tripping samba-like along. The feeling is the
opposite of comic: it is huge, and tragically overrid-
ing; it shadowed her entire life, reaching wherever in
the hemispheres she tried to escape it. The form, al-
most the opposite of the feeling, makes the feeling explor-
able; it is the anchor of the opposite which makes the
feeling approachable and which allows the humor and

the light touch that give the poem its brilliance.

The tension of the lightness of the triplets, the clap-clap-clap of the rhymes festive and absurd as mardi gras, against the depth of the poet's complex feelings about the disoriented animal, give the poem that irridescent confusion of form and content. The triple rhymes create the emotion, while the emotion creates the demand for the triple rhymes in such balance that no other choice would be right. Indeed, in final products no other choice is "right." But the initial choice, to contain, to order, to form, to combat the overwhelming darkness of that abandonment, almost opposes the very feeling it is chosen to express, and therefore it makes a safe vehicle for expression. The verse form almost becomes the arms of comfort in which to express the enormity of emotion. This is how the huge inverted world of carnival, like the huge inverted world of Bishop's mother's absence, can be both invoked and tolerated—and made to seem seamless.

To me, formal verse makes impossible emotions possible. Look at the contrast between the children's laughter and the dark tower of night in Barbara Howes' poem "Early Supper," based on the triolet. Barbara Howes uses the highly repetitive triolet as a stanza form, building up the enormity of night in apposition to the contained repetition of the incredibly strict stanza structure. The containment of this strictness implies a terrifying chaos right from the beginning when the poem talks about children's laugher: "Laughter of children brings/ The kitchen down with laughter./ While the old kettle sings/ Laughter of children brings...." The children's laughter exists in an atmosphere of threat, simply because the verse form that boxes the threat is so small, ornate, and delicately hinged. Thus when the children

are put to bed and the dark tower of night is intro-
duced, the threat is openly acknowledged, and finally
the poem makes sense. Here is the last of its three
stanzas in full:

> They trail upstairs to bed,
> And night is a dark tower.
> The kettle calls: instead
> They trail upstairs to bed,
> Leaving warmth, the coppery-red
> Mood of their carnival hour.
> They trail upstairs to bed,
> And night is a dark tower.

At the opening one almost resists it—what is this
silly poem about kettles and laughter? Too, one almost
resists the Bishop poem in its opening—do we have to
read about this silly dog?—because the containment
has yet to reveal its purpose, or what it contains (ter-
ror, of course).

That observation could quickly lead to the fallacy of
the verse form as a container or the *outside* of some-
thing, and therefore, as an outside, something superfi-
cial, not deep, merely technical. But when I speak of
containment, I am speaking about not being over-
whelmed; I am not speaking about tying something
up in a package to be shelved. I am indicating a po-
etic method of coping with the vastness of emotion
that makes the poem worth writing in the first place.
If you think of form as the outside of an Inside, that is
only half the truth. Verse form is also inside the In-
side. It acts as a skeleton as well as a skin. It is a body.
Verse form literally embodies the emotion of the poem,
in the sense that embodiment both *is* and *contains* the
life it is the body of. The need to embody the danger-
ous is both a need to surround it *and* then to live it.

Therefore the initial choice is to contain and the subsequent writing allows the danger to live as made possible by the containment.

*   *   *   *

How I happened to permit myself to tackle a vast male tradition and also be so playful with it is due, in part, to my female models. I very much wanted to write "real" poetry and to me that usually meant Shakespeare or the Romantics and that always meant emotional. So part of my initial goal was very male-modeled, and naive, too, born of the values engendered by my teachers and of the colossal ambition these values encouraged. I loved the density of the formal enterprise, but the other part of my goal, to express emotion as directly as I could, caused me to shy away from the tyranny of perfection because, for me, emotion had to come first. The reason I loved the formal density is that with each poem I wrote I had to conquer the colossal fear of saying what I felt I could not say. At first it was the fear of the sexually explicit, or the fear of revealing my father's alcoholism, then my position as adult hostage to this early abuse. Finally I realized every subject I was drawn to made me afraid. This continues in my life, and the poem "Devolution" is an example. It's frightening to me to discuss holy communion as the eating of God. I feared throughout the poem that I was transgressing if I discussed my childish idea that eating the host meant eating a part of Jesus—His esophagus? His eyeball? His penis? Elizabeth Bishop's stylistic "imperfections" inspired me. If a rhyme scheme didn't suit her, she dropped it; if she felt like rhyming a syllable with a whole word she playfully hyphenated the word into two lines, and so do I, internalizing her example in "Devolution."

I was delighted once to hear a (probably apocryphal) story that Marianne Moore used colored pencils to keep her sound patterns in place as she wrote. That is the kind of thing I do when I work with learning disabled children, and the kind of very simple system I need for myself. The story permitted me to draw charts of poems, laying them out spatially so that I could concentrate on the emotional complexities without losing the "grid" of the format. I did this in "ChrisEaster," which was very painful to write. Even the broken rhyme scheme I used (a mutilated abab) had to be charted separately before I began the poem. Otherwise, I couldn't have gotten through it.

I always look to female models, "minor" though they are thought to be. One important one is Elinor Wylie's sonnet sequence "Wild Peaches." I felt instantly on reading it that Wylie had started out to write one sonnet and had overrun it into more because she was out of lines but not out of things to say. "Good Girl" takes a bit of Wylie's advice. It's what I would call a heroic sonnet, but "Good Girl" came out unintentionally four lines over because I had more to say—I couldn't contain myself. Through "Wild Peaches" Elinor Wylie released me from the tyranny of fourteen lines, but not the guidance, safety, and mirroring of emotion that form offers. That's just what "Good Girl" is about; by running over I stopped myself from being a good girl to the sonnet.

I began to think of writing poetry as doing needlework: embroidering anything ambitious, however even your stitches, requires you to negotiate tons of mistakes. For instance, "Anger Sweetened" appears to be a perfect sonnet, but my rhyme scheme got away from me. (It goes abbbaaccbddee.) Yet the odd rhyme recurrence easily becomes part of the fabric of the poem. I let this happen intentionally, for the rhymes seemed to be a part of the expression of the anger, their "mistakeness" part of the general mistakeness of repressing anger. Look at quilts or lace or medieval tapestries: for all the perfect skill are the nubs, the sew overs, the piecings together, a revision process allowing for a conglomerate of mistakes and a final, integrated whole. To me that is what craft is.

And that is how I come by my female poetic heritage: Edna Millay smoking cigarettes in sonnets, Christina Rossetti's bald sadness, Charlotte Mew's reconsiderations on the stairs after a party, Louise Bogan's panic made palpable, all showing themselves, their humanity and the femaleness of their emotion through bending the tension of the verse strictures, either in feeling or in form, all making the decision to choose traditional verse and all to alter it to their purposes. In "How I Had To Act" I tell the story of a shopping mistake; I was so interested in getting the narrative out that I didn't set a tight frame for myself. I felt if I rhymed any two lines in a stanza I'd be doing all right, since I wasn't quite sure how it would all turn out. I needed guidance by rhyme, not entrapment; I needed to be able to play.

It is not that men cannot be playful in their formal verse enterprises (I think instantly of Robert Creeley, Philip Larkin, Auden, Richard Wilbur, Richard Howard, and James Merrill) but I often, perhaps wrongly, think of them as admiring rigor more than I do. I feel encouraged by the whimsy, the inexactitude, the changes in the type of containment women poets chose and choose and feel the female embodiment of traditional verse to be altered by a sensibility that acknowledges fluctuation and imperfection, while at the same time it values the interplay between the chaos of emotion and the order of form.

I am making two points really. One is that style is not always consonant with substance, that in fact, form can be chosen in opposition to the magnitude of feeling the poet wishes to evoke and therefore the form can embody its opposite. I do not think that it's particularly linked to one sex or the other, but that it is in the nature of the initial choice of one form over another. The other point is about the tolerance of imperfection in technique that I sense is particularly female, though heaven knows I do not prove this, and only suggest that it is there. Perhaps because it is so true of my own work, I may be generalizing too easily to others'. My aim was to inquire into the making of the beautiful blue-green feather that projects the dazzling confusion of feeling and form in the final product of a poem. This bifurcated into my two points. One was green. One was blue.

CHRISEASTER

I woke up to the bleating of a lamb
in the garagelike recovery room
crowded with wheeled beds waiting to be parked.
  "Am
I?" I asked as I began to disentomb

myself from the anesthesia, "where I am?"
Why is there a lamb in this garagelike farm?

Something was wrong in the barn. The nervous
  bleat-cry
continued. When I raised my head in alarm

and saw the green hospital interior
and felt the blood between my legs and was
frightened, I thought, "It is not hygenic to store
a lamb in here!" Of course the bleating I heard was

a baby crying helplessly way down the room.
I had had an abortion and the baby crying
was someone else's, yet mine—the world was a womb
and the room was still a barn. Lying

back in my stupor in the manger, "ChrisEaster,"
I thought, for it was Eastertime, but I had
condensed the birth and death that were
usually separated by seasons as I bled,

then closed my eyes sarcophagally.
Oh, yes, the lamb was the Lamb of God, bleating
in hunger and terror in the tomb room, all woolly
and soft with human pain. My heart lay beating

steadily, for I was alive. Marc stood weeping
in the hall, and later watched as I lay sleeping
in the manger, on the bald hill, near the tomb
at home.

DEVOLUTION

When the wafer dissolves on my tongue, won-
der what part of the Lord I have eaten,
His scrotum molecularly recon-
structed in a pale disc, or a wheaten
flap of armpit? Perhaps internal organs

vaporized to universal atoms
from the thorax of our Lord. Others had plans
to preserve the saints in bits, the phantom
of Anthony's larynx in a ruby vase,
Agatha's breasts in gold caskets, the flesh
reserved. I only eat our Lord, and mas-
ticate the host, the church a crèche,
and I in my stall not even knowing how
to blow glass housing for a saint or wield
a hammer with my hoof, unable to bow
or scoop breasts into a box. The world
transubstantiates me to animal
evolving in reverse: soon I could be a lizard
on the wall of the manger, in time one-celled,
perhaps a single cell of the baby Lord,
perhaps His tongue, so what I chew as symbol
I might at last become: simple.

HOW I HAD TO ACT

One day I went and bought a fake fur coat
from two old ladies in a discount shop
no young woman should have walked into: taupe

fluff with leopard spots for four hundred bucks
which I charged—no cash till my paycheck—
admired by the two old saleslady crooks.

Five minutes later I was at my shrink's
casually shoving the bag by a chair,
one arm flopping out synthetically. Trinkets,

all belonging to my crooked grandmother,
floated across the wall already filled with the shrink's
trinkets. Afterwards, among the minks

on the street, I caught sight of my grandmother
in a shopwindow. The wind was howling.
I wore the fake coat with a babushka. Another

possibility was: that was *me*. I didn't
have four hundred dollars and felt humiliated
by what I had acted out and berated

myself for buying a blazer in the size
of my sister the week before! You MESS!
I called myself a lot of names. Eyes

on the bus looked up when I barreled on
in the coat I couldn't return to the store.
I refused to go shopping alone anymore.

My rich friend said, "A fun fur... how daring."
How daring to become my clever, lying
grandmother and before that my sister, whose loved,

dirty stuffed leopard Gram craftily destroyed.
I had promised myself a real fur coat
which I wanted as I did a real self, employed

with real feelings. Instead I bought a fake
which I couldn't afford. "What a mistake!"
I chortled to my shrink, who agreed,

though I did not want her to. How terrible,
I wanted her to say, How terrible
you have to act this way.

ANGER SWEETENED

What we don't forget is what we don't say.
I mourn the leaps of anger covered
by quizzical looks, grasshoppers covered

by coagulating chocolate. Each word,
like a leggy thing that would have sprung away,
we caught and candified so it would stay
spindly and alarmed, poised in our presence,
dead, but in the shape of its old essence.
We must eat them now. We must eat the words
we should have let go but preserved, thinking
to hide them. They were as small as insects blinking
in our hands, but now they are stiff and shirred
with sweet to twice their size, so what we gagged
will gag us now that we are so enraged.

GOOD GIRL

Hold up the universe, good girl. Hold up
the tent that is the sky of your world at which
you are the narrow center pole, good girl. Rup-
ture is the enemy. Keep all whole. The itch
to be yourself, plump and bending, below a sky
unending, held up by God forever
is denied by you as Central Control. Sever
yourself, poor false Atlas, poor "Atlesse," lie
recumbent below the sky. Nothing falls down,
except you, luscious and limited on the ground.
Holding everything up, always on your own,
creates a loneliness so profound
you are nothing but a column, good girl,
a temple ruin against a sky held up
by forces beyond you. Let yourself curl
up: a fleshy fetal figure cupped
about its own vibrant soul. You are
the universe about its pole. God's not far.

THE SPELL

The job in certain lives has been to find **A**
way to live with feeling—for just to **B**
the selves they are requires them to **C**
things they were forbidden to. All the **D**
structive or delicious forces became in**E**
luctable vapors inside the in**F**
able masks of personal traits the wee**G**
boards of their parents created. But their n**H**
ures were disguised, not destroyed.

                                        I
have the same job in my life, avoiding the **J**-
hook of Things Not To Say, not to *know* (not ris**K**
things, but life-threatening ones, with their deep w**L**
of being unloved and unforgiven). **M**
pathy was my way out. My mother wouldn't ev**N**
feel anything; she actually unlearned how to (th**O**
feeling what everyone else felt was simply **P**
nal servitude).

                    Generations got this **Q**
from generations: Don't say what you feel, *you* **R**
not you. Generations of liars in a m**S**
one got the next one into became a **T**
leology of undoing. *You are not* **U**,
you must hide what you feel. Behind your **V**
nial mask you must hide, you as a **W**,
as spelling masks meaning, a kind of h**X**
on the alphabet, created to cover **Y**,
not to destroy it, but to make it ha**Z**.

HELEN PINKERTON
True Recovery

My view of form is that it is essential to the art of poetry, both in meter and in rhetorical structure. I have always written in standard English meter, never abandoning it for variations into accentual or syllabic meters, still less for so-called "free verse" or lineated prose. Since about 1950 poetry as an art has nearly been destroyed by the almost universal loss by readers and writers of the perception of the standard English metrical line, as practiced by poets from Chaucer and Shakespeare to Frost, Robinson, Bogan and Winters. Whether poetry as an art can be recovered is questionable, but true recovery can only be based on recovery of the metrical line.

ON DOROTHEA LANGE'S PHOTOGRAPH
"MIGRANT MOTHER" (1936)
(to my Aunt Nora)

Remembering your face, I see it here,
Eyes weary, unexpectant, unresigned.
Not wise, but self-composed and self-contained,
And not self-pitying, you knew how to give
And when to take and, waiting, not despair.
During bitter years, when fear and anger broke
Men without work or property to shadows
(My childhood's world), you, like this living woman,
Endured, keeping your small space fresh and kind.

ON VERMEER'S "YOUNG WOMAN WITH A WATER JUG" (1658) IN THE METROPOLITAN MUSEUM

Not Martha nor Diana—only a woman
Working alone, light falling through the casement
On forearms, yellow jacket, blue-white coif,
On a clear brow and eyes that look within.
She pauses in meditative quiet, conscious
That in her being, before her work resumes,
She sees and she is seen, knows and is known—
Thinking, "It is as if this precious light,
Uniting me and him who looks at me,

Imaged the unsourced being, first and actual,
That gives our being momently, our seeing
And what we see, knowing and what we know.
It is as if my task, privately done,
Its time and place not in the world's arena,
Showed truth beyond geography's fine maps
Or charts of the astronomer—truth needed
By him who paints me here in his bright fiction,
Alone, as he is too, and also not alone."

MARY JO SALTER
A BEAUTIFUL SURFACE

Formalism is one means of "finishing" something.
The crude formalist, the versifier, may count himself
finished once everything rhymes. The better poet seeks
a finish that may employ, but goes beyond, the con-
ventional tools: rhyme, meter, syllabics, stanzas. Poets
who move us write not only to relieve the pressure of
present feelings but to put an end to them. They write
about lost lovers in order to write them off. Even the
warm tribute to restless Spring freezes it. The most
anguished elegy is a polished coffin to silence the poet's
own heart in.

This the reader opens; for him, or her, the poet's
heart beats again. With any luck, readers mistake that
heart for their own. What was finished has begun some-
where else.

It's a tired misapprehension, then, that chains for-
malism to the dead past or to an assumed coolness of
feeling. Nothing unsettles us so much—in poetry, or
people—as a beautiful surface.

CHERNOBYL

Once upon a time,
the word alone was scary.
Now, quainter than this rhyme,
it's the headline of a story

long yellowed in the news.
The streets were hosed in Kiev,

and Poles took more shampoos.
The evacuees were brave.

Under the gay striped awning
of Europe's common market,
half-empty booths were yawning
at the small change in the pocket.

As far away as Rome,
unseen through weeks of sun,
the cloud kept children home.
Milk gurgled down the drain.

In Wales, spring lambs were painted
blue, not to be eaten
till next spring when... Still tainted,
they'd grown into blue mutton.

Then we had had enough.
Fear's harder to retain
than hope or indifference. Safe
and innocent, the rain

fell all night as we slept,
and the story at last was dead—
all traces of it swept
under the earth's green bed.

WHAT DO WOMEN WANT?

"Look! It's a wedding!" At the ice cream shop's
pristine picture window, the fortyish
blonde in the nice-mother shorts and top
stops short to raise two cones, one in each hand,
as if to toast the frothy blur of bride
emerging from St. Brigid's across the green.

"Mom," a boy answers, " I said I want a *dish*."
But this washes under her, while a well-matched band
of aqua-clad attendants pours outside
to laugh among fresh, buttonholed young men.

Young men...remember *them?* Her entourage
now is six boys, and she buys each one his wish.
When she peers up from her purse, the newlyweds
have sped away, and she notices at last,
on the littered steps of the Universalist
Society, some ten yards from St. Brigid's,
a rat-haired old woman in a camouflage
Army-Navy outfit, in whose pockets bulge
rags, or papers, and an unbagged beverage.
Looks like a flask of vodka. But no, it's dish-

washing liquid! It's Ivory, the household god.
The shape is clear from here: a voodoo doll,
headless, with the waist pinched, like a bride.
Poor thing—her dirty secret nothing worse
than the dream of meals to wash up after. While
what *she* most craves, standing at this font
of hope, the soda-fountain, with the boys
all eating hand-to-mouth, is not to miss
the thing that...well, it's hard to say; but what
she'd want, if we were given what we want.

THE REBIRTH OF VENUS

He's knelt to fish her face up from the sidewalk
all morning, and at last some shoppers gather
to see it drawn—wide-eyed, and dry as chalk—
whole from the sea of dreams. It's she. None other

than the other one who's copied in the book
he copies from, that woman men divined

ages before a painter let them look
into the eyes their eyes had had in mind.

Love's called him too, today, though she has taught
him in her beauty to love best
the one who first had formed her from a thought.
One square of pavement, like a headstone (lest

anyone mistake where credit lies),
reads BOTTICELLI, but the long-closed dates
suggest, instead, a view of centuries
coming unbracketed, as if the gates

might swing wide to admit, here, in the sun,
one humble man into the pantheon
older and more exalted than her own.
    Slow gods of Art, late into afternoon

let there be light: a few of us drop the wish
into his glinting coin-box like a well,
remembering the forecast. Yet he won't rush
her finish, though it means she'll have no shell

to harbour in; it's clear enough the rain
will swamp her like a tide, and lion-hearted
he'll set off, black umbrella sprung again,
envisioning faces where the streets have parted.

YOUNG GIRL PEELING APPLES
(Nicholas Maes)

It's all
    an elaborate pun:
the red peel of ribbon
    twisted tightly about the bun
        at the crown of her apple-

round head;
the ribbon coming loose in the real
apple-peel she allows to dangle
from her lifted hand; the table
on which a basket of red

apples
waits to be turned into more
white-fleshed apples in a water-
filled pail on the floor;
her apron that fills and falls

empty,
a lapful of apples piling on
like the apron itself, the napkin,
the hems of her skirts—each a skin
layered over her heart, just as he

who has
painted her at her knife
paints the brush that gives life
to her, apple of his eye: if
there's anything on earth but this

unbroken
concentration, this spiral
of making while unmaking while
the world goes round, neither the girl
nor he has yet looked up, or spoken.

SONIA SANCHEZ
FORM AND RESPONSIBILITY

I am a poet who has from the very beginning written in free verse, but there have been times in my life when I have retreated to form. When I have had to deal with formal pain, I have written in the sonnet. When I have thought I had very little time to put some of my thoughts on paper, I've retreated to haiku and tanka and felt a world of form that allowed me to live and breathe out my pain and joy. When I have been expansive and sassy and wanted to flaunt it and to come off the edge of the paper, I have dealt with the blues, sung the blues, lived the blues, tasted the blues— I have made the blues, I've been the blues.

I first started to study form at N.Y.U. with Louise Bogan, who taught us forms like the sonnet and villanelle. I wrote the "Father and Daughter" poems as sonnets because talking about that formal pain, talking about this very formal man, required a form. The poems began with a line I had left over in a journal from the sonnet-exercise in Louise Bogan's course. I started writing haiku on my own, after I stumbled across a collection of haiku. Haiku gave me room to say what I needed to say in fewer words, and there was a satisfaction from that. At a time when I was very sick and didn't have time to write longer poems, I zeroed in on the haiku. I thought it would be clichéd if I wrote nature haiku, so I delved into it in the sense of making it modern. I had done ballads in the Bogan class, played a lot of blues, listened to a lot of blues, and so I drifted into the blues form also. I like the blues because it has the history of African-American people in it, and it always has sexual undertones that you can play with a great deal.

To this day, I teach form to my undergraduates—haiku and tanka to blues and ballads, etc. Students come into my class and they say, "your politics are so hip and then we get in here and you throw this form at us"; they say, "let's get out of here." I have to explain to them that if you were a runner and I wanted to get you in under four minutes, I'd have to work with you, work on your skills and habits, and with writing it's the same thing; you have to deal with form. I tell them, we all write free verse mostly, but all free verse has form, there is a form there. We assume a line can go anyplace, but once you truly know form, free verse becomes familiar and you understand free verse better.

Young people tend to overwrite; that's why I start with haiku. "That's an easy form," they say. Then they come back the next week and they look at you and say, "That was not as simple as it seemed." They write tanka and cinquains and then they make up their own syllabic verse form (the way I made up my own syllabic verse form, the songku), and then they write free verse. After three weeks of compressed forms, they think they will be able to spread out in free verse. Then they say, "I know why you gave us the forms, because now when I write free verse I look at each word—I examine it, I ask, what is this word doing here." Then I make them write forms for three weeks more before they write free verse again. We study iambic pentameter, and I make them understand that they speak in iambic pentameter.

I began an elegy for my brother in rhyme royal because I was teaching Gwendolyn Brooks' "Anniad." I thought it would be maybe fifteen stanzas. I thought we were always in control, but this piece disproved that; the stanzas kept coming. It kept coming. Then I said, oh, this is not just rhyme royal; I realized it's what I call a neo-slave narrative, about a young African-American man who moves from the south to the north, is alienated in the north, moves towards education, thinking that will free him....You can use form and you can make it do what you want. In this day and age, people are listening to rhyme more, but the form lets rhyme come out in a different way. By using it, I was trying to make the poem ancient and archaic, in a sense, so you understand that this form means giving honor to him.

Form makes you understand that you are responsible for the words you write. I don't feel concerned about any political implications of form. I'm a poet, and the form is not going to form me. I will take the form and say what I want to say; the form will not deform me. Most of all, what I've learned from form is that my free verse has form also. It has taught me that poetry is form and that poetry demands form and discipline, even if we call some of it free verse.

HAIKU
(for paul robeson)

your voice unwrapping
itself from the congo
contagious as shrines.

HAIKU

Was it yesterday
love we shifted the air and
made it blossom Black?

SONG NO. 3
(for 2nd & 3rd grade sisters)

cain't nobody tell me any different
i'm ugly and you know it too
you just smiling to make me feel better
but i see how you stare when nobody's watching you.

i know i'm short black and skinny
and my nose stopped growin fo it wuz' posed to
i know my hairs short, legs and face ashy
and my clothes have holes that run right through to you.

so i sit all day long just by myself
so i jump the sidewalk cracks knowin i cain't fall
cuz who would want to catch someone who looks like me
who ain't even cute or just a little tall.

cain't nobody tell be any different
i'm ugly anybody with sense can see.
but. one day i hope somebody will stop me and say
looka here. a pretty little black girl lookin' just like me.

SONG NO. 2

i say. all you young girls waiting to live
i say. all you young girls taking yo pill
i say. all you sisters tired of standing still
i say. all you sisters thinkin you won't, but you will.

don't let them kill you with their stare
don't let them closet you with no air
don't let them feed you sex piece-meal
don't let them offer you any old deal.

i say. step back sisters. we're rising from the dead
i say. step back johnnies. we're dancing on our heads
i say. step back man. no mo hangin by a thread
i say. step back world. can't let it all go unsaid.

i say. all you young girls molested at ten
i say. all you young girls giving it up again & again
i say. all you sisters hanging out in every den
i say. all you sisters needing your own oxygen.

don't let them trap you with your coke
don't let them treat you like one fat joke
don't let them bleed you till you broke
don't let them blind you in masculine smoke.

i say. step back sisters. we're rising from the dead
i say. step back johnnies. we're dancing on our heads
i say. step back man. no mo hanging by a thread.
i say. step back world. can't let it go unsaid.

FATHER AND DAUGHTER

we talk of light things you and I in this
small house. no winds stir here among
flame orange drapes that drape our genesis
And snow melts into rivers. The young
grandchild reviews her impudence that
makes you laugh and clap for more allure.
Ah, how she twirls the emerald lariat.
When evening comes your eyes transfer
to space you have not known and taste the blood
breath of a final flower. Past equal birth,

the smell of salt begins another flood:
your land is in the ashes of the South.
perhaps the color of our losses:
perhaps the memory that dreams nurse:
old man, we do not speak of crosses.

MAY SARTON
WHERE THE GREATEST MYSTERY LIES

I have said that form is earned. What I mean by that is that the music of a poem does not show itself unless one's whole being is at a high pitch of concentration. The experience base of the poem must have been revelatory. The trouble with free verse is that very rarely (D. H. Lawrence comes to mind as an exception) does the intensity seem great enough; the danger is the diffuse, self-indulgent, not closely enough examined content.

If the pressure base of the poem is great enough, then I find almost always that among those rough chaotic notes I jot down in the moment of inspiration, there is one line that suggests meter, and sometimes I can sense the whole first stanza. It is here in the music of the poem that the greatest mystery lies. I suppose that a practising poet has inside him the rumor of many sounds, the patterns of poems by others which he has totally absorbed. He doesn't say—ever—that he is going to write a sonnet; he has a sonnet idea; a sonnet hums inside this idea, and the form is inevitable if it is to be valid. We do not impose form on the poem; form is organic. But just as with the image, the poet in a state of inspiration may go wrong unless he is extremely self-critical. The enemies of creation are and have always been facility, cleverness, self-indulgence, and above all a misunderstanding about what inspiration is. I know that I am inspired when I become a fury of self-criticism to dig out what I really mean from a lot of irrelevancies that have poured down on the page in the first excitement of the start.

SMALL JOYS
New Year, 1990

What memory keeps fresh, frames unspoken,
I catch for you, innumerable friends.
When so much else has been destroyed or broken
These joys remain intact as the year ends,
A year of earth-grief and of bitter news,
The starving children and the burning trees,
Otters coated in oil and dolphins drowned.
Small joys keep life alive. I give you these.
They will not die, you know. They stay around.

When the long winter lingered on
And all the color stayed an ugly brown,
Suddenly snowdrops had pushed their way through
And their sharp whiteness made all new.

Early in February owls began to woo,
Their language gentle, calling "Who? Who? Who?"
And I was lit up when an awesome bird
In the harsh cold spoke such a tender word.

The finches changed their suits early this year
From olive to bright gold, and there they were
Burbling as always, their busy flight a whir
Of yellow weaving through static air.

The daffodils in April thronged the grass
And all along the wood's edge, fabulous
To show the thousand faces of a nation,
Expected, still beyond all expectation.

Later in June, alive with silent fire,
The fireflies pulsed their firefly desire
And from the terrace I could watch the dance,
Follow their bliss. It happened only once.

Full summer brought nasturtiums in profusion.
I picked and bent to drink the sweet confusion,
Yellow and orange, the fresh scent. I could
Keep summer in a bowl for days, and did.

One autumn night my cat ran to my call
And leapt five feet over the terrace wall.
A second, weightless, he flowed and did not fall
That silver splendor, princely and casual.

And last I give you murmur of waves breaking,
The sound of sleep that is a kind of waking
As the tide rises from the distant ocean
And all is still and yet all in motion.

The small joys last and even outlast earthquake.
I give you these for love—and for hope's sake.

THE TORTURED

Cried Innocence, "Mother, my thumbs, my thumbs!
The pain will make me wild."
And Wisdom answered, "Your brother-man
Is suffering, my child."

Screamed Innocence, "Mother, my eyes, my eyes!
Someone is blinding me."
And Wisdom answered, "Those are your brother's eyes,
The blinded one is he."

Cried Innocence, "Mother, my heart, my heart!
It bursts with agony."
And Wisdom answered, "That is your brother's heart
Breaking upon a tree."

Screamed Innocence, "Mother, I want to die.
I cannot bear the pain."

And Wisdom answered, "They will not let him die.
They bring him back again."

Cried Innocence, "Mother, I cannot bear
It now. My flesh is wild!"
And Wisdom answered, "His agony is endless
For your sake, my child."

Then whispered Innocence, "Mother, forgive,
Forgive my sin, forgive—"
And Wisdom wept. "Now do you understand, Love,
How you must live?"

MAUREEN SEATON
HONORING THE SONNET

A first teacher once told me: "You'll never be a son-neteer, Maureen." This after my initial attempts to break from traditional rhyme and rhythm, that predictable punctuation at the end of ten-syllable lines. But I never aspired to sonneteer although I love the tradition. I simply enjoyed making puzzles for myself to solve, employing tension to heighten language, stretching the form until it fell apart or became something new.

After hundreds of sonnets I began to discover (com-paratively) enormous block-like poems that enable me to tell stories the way I like to. And I honor the son-net, its ability to reduce a novel to a single paragraph, that play within a rhythm so natural to the English language. It's been a transformative vehicle for me, a joy, satisfying the way all discovery can be. So thanks to the teacher who said I couldn't. And to Marilyn Hacker, the one who said I could.

FEAR OF SUBWAYS
(from "Sonnets for a Single Mother")

Sometimes in the dark I fear trampling,
an effortless extinction of the spirit
underground: mass transit overflowing
onto dangerous edges of piers. It
connects palpably to suffocation,
a child's version of rape, vapid plots
of war movies—but who's the victim?
I used to envy the unrapable, not

for any powermad apparatus curled
benignly in the bathwater, but for his
fortunate position outside of harm.
Or so I thought. Until the old man's arm
caught between the doors of the F train, his
mouth so close to mine I smelled his world.

FEAR OF SHOPLIFTING
(from "Sonnets for a Single Mother")

I've two teenage daughters, a decent
view of Hudson in winter, no regrets.
I'm too proud to accept support, yet men
seem to fear me. My daughters steal rent
and forage for the icebox with the G
missing from the GE and no egg slots.
Once, I saw my right hand lift a ten-spot
from the drawer at work where they trust me.
I kept it several weeks to see how
it would feel, but it smoldered inside.
My daughters laugh as they empty pockets
of hairspray and double-A batteries, trinkets
no young American should live without—
whatever society provides.

WINGS

"Angels Really Exist and Thousands See Them,"
Sun, July 31, '90

In a highly classified report smuggled
out of Russia, three cosmonauts admit
to seeing angels while in orbit.
Country Western singer Johnny Cash said
he'd seen them twice, both times warning him

of death. Who wouldn't believe old Johnny,
or grown men trapped in space, or testimony
of a three-year-old girl with fever? Whim
or fantasy aside, would a woman
tumbling down an icy slope lie?
What's wrong with believing in angels
when the alternative is a wingless
society of hell-bent humans
too silly or senseless to know not to die?

LESLIE SIMON
ON "STREET BLEATS"

"Street Bleats," a series of poems inspired by the names of San Francisco streets, evolved organically from the simple circumstance of writing out invitations to a party on Manchester Street in my San Francisco neighborhood. The directions, "Take Bessie to Manchester," written over and over again on each of fifteen or twenty postcards (why I didn't avail myself of xerox, scissors and paste only the Muse knows), started a kind of song inside of me. The first poem in the series, "Taking Bessie to Manchester," was born. It followed naturally from hand to head.

Not meant to be imitation Gertrude Stein, "Street Bleats" merely suggest elements of her style. And the jazz of the city, any big city—another friendly presence—works its way into the rhythms of these poems. The jagged starts and stops, corners and meetings, and promising intersections embedded in these lines love the simple rhymes of this form. Repeat and revise, as they say.

HATTIE WENT TO MARKET

A biscuit, a basket. Hattie went to Market.

(Let Hattie be a prostitute, a call girl, or just an independent woman.)

a bliss it, a kiss it. Hattie said, "you can sniff it.

"just don't rip it, or rape it, or trap it, or take it.

"don't lock it or mock it. Don't defame it or maim it."

such a sweet cake. a treat cake.

she baked it. she made it.

Hattie went to Market.

NELLIE GIVES INTO BLANCHE

Nellie named her Blanche for white and French. two things she never was. because. because she thought her girl would curl. her girl would curl another time. another time and place.

her face. was black.

her hair was thick. she never hid her looks. she took them where she went. and loved herself in health. she loved herself in health.

the beauty that she was. because. because she was herself. wherever that she went. she lent. her beauty where she went.

her mother gave her love a dove. she gave her love a dove. called it white and Blanche.

her daughter found another bird. she called it black and raven. she found her own. she found her own sky haven.

"mother, don't you see," she said. "I'm your girl, but I curl around another time and place. my face is mine and fine. my face is very fine."

her mother turned to look. she saw a sparkle. there. and so, a glow. "I know," she said, "your face is yours and fine. your face is very fine."

Nellie gives into Blanche.

BERNICE GOT NEXT TO ISIS

something for her lips. oh dare, oh share. something for her lips.

a lick of chord to horde. a gentle slice of flesh be blessed.

the street's in heat, discreet. the street's in heat. bottles bunched, bouquet-like at her curbs.

a wonder, that thunder.

the very angle of her eye. what lie between her sigh. the very angle of her eye. oh my. oh thigh. oh, oh hi!

iron and dust. metal and lust. they sly. they sly.

Bernice got next to Isis.

ELIZABETH SPIRES
SOME NOTES ON FORM

Despite the poetry "wars" of the eighties that raged between some of my contemporaries, I have never felt the necessity to choose, in some absolute sense, between form and free verse. Neither have some of the poets of the preceding two generations whom I most admire and who, at one time or another, have been poetic models for my own work—poets such as Elizabeth Bishop, Anthony Hecht, and W.D. Snodgrass, to name just three.

In my own poems, I have always let the early drafts of a poem lead me, when they would, to a fixed rhyme scheme, an approximate line length, a metrical base (or the opposite—free verse lineation, etc.) rather than deciding beforehand, the poem unwritten, what form I would work in. Of the three poems reprinted here, "Apology" is probably the most "formal." It is a poem about limits, the unhappy limits of a life, the short set stanzas and line lengths meant to reinforce a sense of confinement. The identical rhymes used in the quatrains culminate, I hope, in a kind of "dead-end" effect in the last stanza with the poem's final assertion: "A song is narrow. A life is narrow." An obsessive, circling quality is present in the use of the refrain, "Who am I? Who am I like?" in "Interrogations of the Sparrow." In these poems the form chosen, I hope, creates a kind of "inverted" lyric moment not of praise or affirmation but of mental and physical entrapment of the speaker.

I've probably taken the most liberties with "The Comb

and the Mirror," a narrative poem that I imagine a poet of a more formal bent would have written as a ballad. Instead, I opted for a three-beat iambic line with occasional trochaic substitution to give the poem a slightly off-balance, asymmetrical quality. My justification for this resides in the speaker, a mermaid straddling her world of water and the alien world of her human lover. In certain passages, I knew I wanted the phrasing to be slightly unnatural or inverted, the syntax mirroring the mermaid's own awkwardness on land and her pain and ambivalence in retelling the story.

My tendency when reading my contemporaries (as well as in reacting to my own students' poems) is to wish that diehard formalists would sometimes "loosen" the ties that bind them and that militant advocates of free verse would occasionally experiment with set forms. To limit ourselves as poets to either form or free verse exclusively is to narrow our expressive possibilities both in terms of what subjects we will write about and how that subject matter will be treated. Personally, I am hoping that the poetry wars of the 1980's have ended and that we can all just settle down and write, in the nineties, without proscriptions or dogmatism, the best poems we are capable of.

THE COMB AND THE MIRROR
Based on the Cornish folktale of the mermaid of Zennor

Two-natured, loving my world
but loving you as much,
I came every seventh day
to lonely Zennor parish
and hid outside the church.
From fish to forked human,

changing my form I came,
to hear you, Mathey Trewhella,
nakedly sing your hymns;
I drowned in the songs you sang.
Week after week I returned,
until Highsummer Sunday
you spied my lovesick face
in the church's great glass window,
a stranger among the saints.
On new unsteady legs
I tried to run away,
not wanting you to net me,
but you followed anyway,
or would in vain have followed.
Held back by humankind
(they warned you of my charms),
you thought but didn't say,
Love cannot help itself.
O bitterly they tell,
bitter to lose one of theirs,
how moonlit nights you searched,
moonstruck and bewitched,
the caves of Pendour Cove
for my flashing mermaid's mirror.
Waist-deep you waded in,
down Neptune's Steps you walked,
and only thought one thought,
Love cannot help itself.
As I myself found out.
Night after night, they tell
how I wrap you in my hair
and we drown in love's delight,
how you like to comb my hair
with a comb of tortoise shell.
Or so the fishwives swear.
But I revise their tale.
Down Neptune's Steps you walked,
backward I swam and you followed,

no spell used I, no words,
to take you to deep depths
where self gives back the self
in love's unreflecting mirror.
Netted unlike to like,
we spent one night together
before a chill dawn broke
and washed away the dream.
I woke in waves and found
my arms around you, drowned.
Never now on earth,
I swear a lover's oath,
shall pairs of lovers find
such harmony of mind
as we for one night shared;
by my heartless comb and mirror,
I will that man and wife
—jealous, mortal, proud—
shall see love turn to spite,
their first love not survive
the weather of their lives.

APOLOGY

Too many nights
the heart cries out,
at first so softly,
calling so softly.

Then all is quiet,
the eye's second sight
adjusts to the darkness,
interior darkness.

The white-throated sparrow
outside the window

stirs once in its sleep,
then exhaustedly sleeps.

All day it sang
the same five notes:
Sorry, so sorry.
Why is it sorry?

Why do the blameless
apologize?
It did nothing wrong.
No, nothing is wrong.

It sings what it knows
but the heart still replies:
A song is narrow.
A life is narrow.

INTERROGATIONS OF THE SPARROW

All night, all night,
I lie on my pallet of straw.
All night, all night,
I hear its white-throated call.
Who am I? Who am I like?

A voice outside the window
hides in the holly tree.
It talks to itself without stopping.
Or does it talk to me?
Who am I? Who am I like?

In a dream I walked in a forest,
pulled by the sparrow's cry,
a shade among white shadows,
a shadow among flickering trees.
Who am I? Who am I like?

A voice as soft as a feather
moved closer, then farther away.
Which tree was the tree of my sparrow?
Would I find it by break of day?
Who am I? Who am I like?

I fell to my knees like a beggar.
I had no pride nor shame.
Holding each tree like a lover,
I begged to know its name.
Who am I? Who am I like?

But each tree withheld an answer,
my cheek only scraped rough bark,
the sparrow heart I was seeking
flying from dark to dark.
Who am I? Who am I like?

Unanswerable question,
I'll answer with my life.
Who am I? Who am I like?
If I knew how I'd sing:
Like no one. No one thing.

MAURA STANTON
REFLECTIONS ON METER

I used to wonder why Shakespeare sounded like Shakespeare and Milton sounded like Milton. I wanted to sound like that, too. I wanted to sound like Chaucer and Keats and Dickinson and Frost and Bishop. They all had their own voices, of course, and no one could ever confuse them with one another, but they all had a driving power in their lines of poetry, and it was that power that I wanted. But I also wanted to sound like me. I have a flat Midwestern accent, and instinct told me that I shouldn't try to lose it in order to sound like a fake Elizabethan or fake Romantic or fake New Englander. So I studied the mystery of their lines, and it was a surprisingly long time after I'd begun writing poetry that I realized the secret was that they all wrote in meter—not the textbook meter of abstract feet that turned poetry into algebra, but in the natural stressed meter of the English language that approximated speech.

So one day, after years of writing in a controlled free verse that accidentally fell into meter at times, I sat down to deliberately write a hundred lines of blank verse. It was a turning point in my life. I felt that I was speaking in my own voice, but that at the same time a deeper force was shaping my lines and giving me a mysterious new entry into my imagination.

I read some books after that, because I wanted to understand what I was doing. For me the most useful definition of meter is the one in John Thompson's little book, *The Founding of English Meter* (Columbia University Press, 1966). Thompson says that meter is made by abstracting from speech one of the essential features of the language—stress—and ordering it into a pattern. The pattern is an imitation of the pattern that stress makes in speech, a sort of formalizing of the pattern. The pattern follows the principles of the language—it's a symbolic model of the way English works.

So what's it for? Thompson says meter does for language what the forms of any art do for their materials. It abstracts certain elements from the experience of the senses and forms them into patterns, as painting abstracts elements from what the eye perceives, dancing from what the body perceives as it moves, as fiction abstracts the events of life into a plot. What meter adds to the language is the element of imitation that makes art. When the metrical pattern is placed in conjunction with some words or phrases, a tension exists between them. The meter exerts a pull on the natural-sound pattern of the phrases.

To abstract the natural stress pattern of English, and to juxtapose it against the ordinary American talk of somebody stuck in a particular place or situation, is one way of creating meaning in a poem—not the only way, of course, but for me it's a way that connects me to the poetry of the past, and allows me to dream of the poetry of the future.

BALLAD OF THE MAGIC GLASSES

"Here are your magic glasses.
  The frames are iron rings.
The adamantine lenses
  Will make your eyes sting."

She put her claw on my arm.
   She put her mouth to my ear.
I nodded while I listened,
   Trembling and pale with fear.

"Look at yourself," she said,
   "Stripped of your delusions.
But never at other people.
   Allow them their illusions."

The glasses fit my face.
   They felt as light as air,
Charmed to be invisible.
   No one could see them there.

Yet anyone looking closely
   Might have thought, "Strange,
Her face is stiff, distorted—"
   And wondered at the change.

I looked into the mirror.
   My true self looked back,
Exposed like a skeleton.
   The glass appeared to crack.

All my darkest motives
   Shone in the eerie light.
My heart was full of worms;
   My lips were sharp with spite.

"Let me repeat my warning,"
   Whispered the old crone
As I gasped at my X-ray vision.
   "These are for you alone."

"Never wear these glasses
   In the company of others.
Never put them on
   In front of friends or lovers."

"Now pay me," she said. "Pay me.
　I want your lovely hair,
I want that unlined skin
　　Around your eyes to wear."

"In return, you have knowledge,
　Bitter, black, weighty,
All you'd acquire later
　　If you lived to be eighty."

I gave her the full price.
　I looked ten years older
Leaving her dingy shop.
　　The day had turned colder.

I felt angry and cheated
　By the high price of Insight,
Since I couldn't use my glasses
　　Except alone at night.

Surrounded by my friends,
　Laughter, smiles and wine,
I wanted another soul
　　On which to brood than mine.

Why should an old crone
　Tell me what to do,
And warn me against that knowledge
　　When I could have it, too?

And so I slipped on my glasses,
　Eager to peer and spy
Beyond the cheerful chatter,
　　To see each naked lie.

My hand grew scaly, and curled
    Around my silver knife
As oily smoke puffed out
    And I saw the inner life.

Poisonous snakes were writhing
    Off every bantering tongue,
While flies hatched in brains
    Constructed out of dung.

Every hand was a hook,
    And every heart a trap
Lined with oozing juices
    To catch some unwary rat.

This friend burned with lust,
    This friend dreamed of cocaine,
This friend envied me,
    This friend felt disdain.

I couldn't distinguish myself
    From the table of beasts—
Jaws, mandibles, tusks.
    My horror increased.

Was everyone just like me?
    I looked down at my plate
Then back at my shocking friends.
    I understood my fate

As I tried to remove my glasses,
    For the frames stuck to my face,
Welded to temple and nose.
    The lenses stayed in place.

I hurried through the streets
   Looking for the crone.
Her shop had disappeared.
   Her vision was my own.

No flower can delight me,
   No singing bird, no sky—
Doomed to wear iron glasses
   Until the day I die.

LIVING APART

I leave our house, our town, familiar fields
Below me at takeoff when I fly to you
Deep in these shadowed mountains. Now at dawn
I wake to the horse-clop of passing carriages
As if I'd passed through time as well as space.
Yesterday we saw an Amish farmer
Bearded and calm, stroking his horse's mane
Under a flaming maple as he watched
Hang-gliders drifting down from Hyner View.
We stopped to watch them, too. I was amazed
To see men falling toward the scarlet treetops
On outspread wings. That's when I grabbed your hand
To tell myself we were alive and human
Not lost in hell which must resemble this—
A place where souls from many centuries
Stand side by side, united but unhappy,
To watch the angels fall from fiery mountains.

PATRICIA STORACE
A Singular Presence

I don't always use traditional stanza forms and metres, and I don't think of myself as a "formalist." But when I do, I find a range of different, and sometimes obscurely related motives in making use of these techniques. I love vocal music, and am as voice-activated as any telephone answering machine ever was; occasionally I write poems with very particular voices in mind, and the use of a particular rhyme scheme or rhythm or stanza pattern is the result of the impression of a person's voice.

And of course, there is the sheer sensual pleasure of the flavors of different patternings—the way two words can seem to rhyme as if they have met in a fatal clash, or can rhyme with an endlessness as if they were in love, the geography of different stanzas, as distinctive to move around in as Oregon is from Martha's Vineyard.

I value the way formal patterns introduce a singular presence into a piece which is not the poet's own presence; they help remind the poet and the reader that the poem is of the world, not the world itself; they bring an element of otherness to the poem which the poet must encounter as independent of her own voice. Something of the condition of life itself enters into the poem, in the act of finding a way to think freely within pre-existing patterns. My use of traditional formal patterns in verse signifies for me the presence of history in the poem, the voice of memory, a powerful presence for me in this art which has from its beginning been preoccupied with the nature of memory.

THE ARCHAEOLOGY OF DIVORCE

We examine today not sacked cities, but sacked lives.
We have studied destruction on a larger scale.
Now we turn to the war between female and male,
the wounds delivered by husbands and wives.

Sir: You really think these failures are related?
Yes, Klein, I have seen impregnable city walls
brought down by convulsions in trivial halls
and cannot think my ideas outdated.

We proceed to the objects salvaged from downstairs.
Shards of the bedroom have their strong appeal,
I admit, but what we find here may help reveal
another aspect of this savage pair.

We assume the couple used to dine in this space.
I emphasize a fact undergraduates may miss—
the same mouths share bread as vulnerably as kiss;
that board, like their bed, brought them face to face.

Here is the table; note these fine archaic knives.
The flesh we scraped from one might indicate
a practice occurring even at this date:
perhaps the two ate each other alive.

At any rate, a struggle: the outcome isn't known.
Look, the chairs overturned in terrible haste,
the bowl of fruit left to rot and waste,
and this carcass of love, gnawed to the bone.

WEDDING SONG

I

Earth in her mercy permits us to repeat
the words that fit the only truth we know,
from his hands, between her breasts, all things grow.

Earth in her mercy permits us to repeat
these acts when consecrate couples meet,
the words that fit the only truth we know,
from his hands, between her breasts, all things grow.

Earth in her mercy permits us to repeat
these acts when consecrate couples meet,
and reap from old sentences like harvest wheat,
the words that fit the only truth we know,
from his hands, between her breasts, all things grow.

II

Listen: a door closes now and tells an end
no one may enter but the married pair,
none challenge holy privacy, or ask a share.

Listen: a door closes now, and tells an end
with fresh soil to till, new fire to tend,
No one may enter but the married pair,
None challenge holy privacy, or ask a share.

Listen: a door closes now, and tells an end
with fresh soil to till, new fire to tend,
neither father, mother, nor beloved friend,
No one may enter but the married pair,
None challenge holy privacy, or ask a share.

III

So male stars and female end their exile,
and fuse and form in wedding life to life,
that human constellation, man and wife.

So male stars and female end their exile,
accept the union that completes their trial,
and fuse and form in wedding life to life,
that human constellation, man and wife.

So male stars and female end their exile,
begin the crossing of their brilliant mile,
accept the union that completes their trial,
and fuse and form in wedding life to life,
that human constellation, man and wife.

KING LEAR BEWILDERED

The leaves are storm-rattled jester's bells
and the king without a court goes courting—
glass chips, lead slivers, seeds in a gourd,
a churning debris in his jester pulse.

*And the lacerating gale, tough-thrashing, is leather
on flesh, as he looks for his girls,
trampling the spongy, pubic heather.*

Oh my body, girl-child, lashed here this ugly night,
shall I lead you out of rain, little one shall I carry you,
I'll dry your soft hair, daughter, the strange snow
drifting on my chest, knotted, now so weirdly white.

*When the mushroom rose between my legs,
I fungus-fathered three, three
fertile daughters. Not one of them can bear me.*

MONA VAN DUYN
OUT-OF-BODY CONCENTRATION

My love of poetry came from nursery rhymes and continued to be nourished on the rhymed verse in school anthologies of that day; college reading offered me an alternative love in the earlier surge of free-verse fashion, which included Whitman, Masters, Sandburg, A. Lowell, H.D., and others, and I have continued to write in both forms, according to the whim of the poem at hand. But I confess to a preference for the poem that comes to me expressing, by whatever mysterious means— the donnée of a line, a vague sense of musical pattern, a nudge of the will to collaborate appropriately with an "idea," or something unanalyzable—a wish to be formal. Why? A friend's son who has recently begun to write stories said in surprise and wonder, "It's the most satisfying thing you can do all by yourself," thereby speaking for us all, it seemed to me. For me, writing a formal poem increases that satisfaction by deepening and intensifying the out-of-body concentration, with its little flares of joy when the right word comes, which we all seek and find in writing poems of whatever kind....

When one spends many years of one's life in small towns, even though one is a reader-writer, one's use-vocabulary normally is small and plain. In a city, one may communicate daily with like-minded people, and also employ speech for jostling, competing with, insulting, swaying others. In small towns, where one must spend close daily life with unchosen fellows, the major use of speech is to accommodate. A small-town reader-writer has an island of use-vocabulary, set in a vast sea of recognition vocabulary, which using rhyme forces him to embark upon. Words that he loves, but that do not readily come to mind for use, are found by rowing out after rhyme. Free verse, which draws from the island of speech, does not force this quest. Concentration is also deepened by the constraints of meter, of course, with its constant questions of when to be regular, when to open up the foot, and so on. As a result, I can freely leave an unfinished free-verse poem to prepare a meal, sleep, have a drink with friends, but a formal poem seems to follow me everywhere, makes me hard to live with, and gives me pleasure approaching the ecstatic.

HOMEWORK
(for Jim)

Lest the fair cheeks begin their shrivelling
before a keeping eye has lit on their fairness,
I pluck from the stony world some that can't cling
to stone, for a homely, transparent form to bless.

Smothering Elbertas, if not Albertines,
in the thick, scalding sweetness of my care,
I add a touch of tart malice, some spicy scenes
and stirring, and screw the lid on love's breathless jar.

There in a frieze they stand, and there they can stay
until, in the fickle world's or the jaded heart's
hunger for freshness, they are consumed away.
Oh I know, I know that, great or humble, the arts

in their helplessness can save but a few selves
by such disguises from Time's hideous bite,
and yet, a sweating Proust of the pantry shelves,
I cupboard these pickled peaches in Time's despite.

THE VISION TEST

My driver's license is lapsing and so I appear
in a roomful of waiting others and get in line.
I must master a lighted box of far or near,
a highway language of shape, squiggle and sign.
As the quarter-hours pass I watch the lady in charge
of the test, and think how patient, how slow, how nice
she is, a kindly priestess indeed, her large,
round face, her vanilla pudding, baked-apple-and-spice
face in continual smiles as she calls each "Dear"
and "Honey" and shows first-timers what to see.
She enjoys her job, how pleasant to be in her care
rather than brute little bureaucrat or saleslady.
I imagine her life as a tender placing of hands
on her children's hands as they come to grips with the rocks
and scissors of the world. The girl before me stands
in a glow of good feeling. I take my place at the box.
"And how are *you* this lovely morning, Dear?
A few little questions first. Your name?— Your age?—
Your profession?" "Poet." "What?" She didn't hear.
"Poet," I say loudly. The blank pink page
of her face is lifted to me. "*What?*" she says.
"POET," I yell, "P-O-E-T."
A moment's silence. "*Poet?*" she asks. "Yes."
Her pencil's still. She turns away from me
to the waiting crowd, tips back her head like a hen
drinking clotted milk, and her "Ha ha hee hee hee"
of hysterical laughter rings through the room. Again
"Oh, ha ha ha ha ha hee hee."
People stop chatting. A few titter. It's clear
I've told some marvelous joke they didn't quite catch.
She resettles her glasses, pulls herself together,
pats her waves. The others listen and watch.
"And what are we going to call the color of your hair?"
she asks me warily. Perhaps it's turned white
on the instant, or green is the color poets declare,

or perhaps I've merely made her distrust her sight.
"Up to now it's always been brown." Her pencil
   trembles,
then with an almost comically obvious show
of reluctance she lets me look in her box of symbols
for normal people who know where they want to go.

SONNET FOR MINIMALISTS

From a new peony,
my last anthem,
a squirrel in glee
broke the budded stem.
I thought, where is joy
without fresh bloom,
that old heart's ploy
to mask the tomb?

Then a volunteer
stalk sprung from sour
bird-drop this year
burst in frantic flower.

The world's perverse,
but it could be worse.

ALMA LUZ VILLANUEVA
THE WIND AND LIGHT

From the beginning, poetry has saved my life. This isn't a metaphor—this is a fact. I began writing poetry after my grandmother's death. My first experience with poetry was seeing/hearing my grandmother recite poetry on the stage in church in a loud, strong, clear voice in Spanish. So, for me, poetry has her voice.*

Poems gather in my womb; then the first line is heard; imagery flows to me, the words become music; music becomes meaning. Then, I know. All that time I'd been filling up with a longing to know, and then I write words "I" wouldn't write. I am answered. Yet it is I. Me. My self.

Technically speaking, I trust the voice of poetry first— feeling, emotion, content, memory. Once it's down on paper a more intellectual part of me, The Critic, The Perfectionist, comes into play, and I use the word "play" rather than "take over" because if The Critic took over I'd never send anything out "finished." So, we play and I accept this and I reject that and then, finally, the poem is itself.

And then each poem has its own unique form—the way the wind and light will emphasize each line, space, word. The Creator, in my body, decides on form instinctively, and The Critic improves or disapproves, and I, between them, hang onto the energy of their play, my longing. In this way the poem is born.

*Though my grandmother, Jesus, was a Christian and married a Baptist minister (who was, also, a poet), she was a full-blood Yaqui Indian from Sonora, Mexico. She came to this

country in her mid-thirties, with a deep Indian reverence to
the Virgin, the Goddess. I also remember her daily chants,
poems, to the rising sun and the setting sun, the first star.

PEACE #3

Is this peace? Kayaking through
the water with a man I do not
love.

Is this peace? Watching a well-fed,
fearless, white-headed otter spin in
seaweed.

Is this peace? Breathing softly as steel
grey pelicans blend and swoop through
fog.

Is this peace? Sitting at sunset with
my nine-year-old son making up nonsense words,
laughing?

Is this peace? The fierce, dark owl perched
on a branch, the horizon burns as she
plunges.

Is this peace? Wondering if it's love, or the lack
of it, that ceases to desire what I do not
possess.

EVEN THE EAGLES MUST GATHER

I lay with an acupuncture needle
at the top of my head
and the Berlin Wall goes down—

I lay with an acupuncture needle
in my left hand pulse
and Prague is free—

I lay with an acupuncture needle
in my right hand pulse
and Mandela walks into sunlight—

I lay with an acupuncture needle
in my left foot pulse
and Russia yearns for commercialism—

I lay with an acupuncture needle
in my right foot pulse
and Chile leans toward democracy—

I send my best energy through my body
in spite of the usual human obstacles—
my spirit is too pure for me, as my body
struggles toward its light-streaked path—

but then, my spirit is all I truly trust
and so I entice it back, I say, "Fill me
up with your pure potential—freedom before
death is what I want, the circle—"

It's afternoon, after a storm, wind
that clears dead branches from trees—
the sun sets—the world seeks its freedom
in its own slow way—we kill the enemy,

make love to the enemy, again and again—
it's the way of transcendence. I look out
the window and despise the cars, the circling
traffic and realize, peace in my body;

Even the eagles must gather (to love
the spirit is to love the body—to love
the earth is to love the world—to love
the enemy is to love the self).

ANNE WALDMAN
SHIFTING CONTEXTS

There are two places the writing delivers itself from: inside and out. Propelling forward or responding back. An arena exists between these polar opposites (inside/ outside, subjective/objective), and the energy of the poem can vibrate from any region within it. From the objective point of view, I often just tell what I see, hear, and know. Another category under the "objective" umbrella is the work with forms: pantoums, sestinas, ghazals, sonnets, cut-ups, canzone, haikun, doha. Where the form dictates the poem by providing an external structure.

The pantoum's ostensible simplicity is deceptive. A pantoum is originally a Malayan form ("pantun" in Malayan), which appeared in the fifteenth century in Malayan literature. It had earlier oral roots and most probably originated in India. Making up pantoums was a popular art and Malayans knew the most famous ones by heart. The Western version of the pantoum is a poem of indefinite length made of four-line stanzas, whose four lines are repeated in a pattern: lines two and four of each stanza are repeated as lines one and three of the next stanza. In the final stanza the second and fourth lines are the same as the third and first lines of the opening stanza (rhyme is optional). The pleasure of the form could be how the context of each line shifts in its relation to the next. This is difficult to achieve. In the past I would start the poem lose the flow and be frustrated by the strain of repetition. It's easy to write an endless chant poem proclaiming "I am a this woman I am a that woman," and yet when it comes to repeating the same six words seven times in a sestina or the same phrases twice in a pantoum they sound strained, confined, wooden, tedious.

When I wrote "Baby's Pantoum" I had been spending most of my time with my infant son in a small cabin in the mountains outside Boulder, Colorado. The father of the child was away working much of the day. I lived inside long twilight days in which I was highly attuned to the way the baby was discovering the world; any mother will tell you this—how they relive creation through a newborn babe. And the environment was minimal, functional, in the service of the baby. There was not a lot of clutter in the house or in our lives. So it was very late the only time there is any time to write when you have a baby and I wanted a gift (as Christmas was coming) for the father of the child and tackled again the pantoum which hadn't been working for me for a number of years. I began writing in the voice of the baby, it was natural to do this, and I was writing in longhand rather than typing to avoid waking the baby, and into the third stanza the problem of the "form" had vanished and the poem began to flow through me. "I" couldn't (because I was the baby speaking) get fancy in my vocabulary. I found the repetitive structure of the pantoum conducive to expressing the baby's thought process. The pantoum lends itself to the idea of the experience of the baby's mind working. The baby's mind would observe things in a series of unconnected glimpses and realizations. Because each line has to be repeated in another context, it's difficult not to have every line be a single phrase or statement. In an older person that might get artificial or coy. Here, single thoughts in the blue don't refer back to a self conscious body of knowledge. So the pantoum became the primary observations of an empty mind, a new arrival. These lines are obviously not what's going on in the baby's mind, but a projection that felt accurate. I felt myself to be a kind of conduit for the baby. The music of the poem was working. I spoke the lines as I wrote. What filled the form, the things said, or seen, were the details of the life going on in the cabin. Every action in the care of the baby is ritualized. The same tasks are performed again and again. The baby is held and rocked and shown the same objects and images, the baby is bathed regularly, the baby is nursed every few hours and so on. The repetitions reflected in the poem were the natural conditions of our daily existence.

BABY'S PANTOUM
(for Reed Bye)

I lie in my crib midday this is
unusual I don't sleep really
Mamma's sweeping or else boiling water for tea
Other sounds are creak of chair & floor, water
dripping on heater from laundry, cat licking itself

Unusual I don't sleep really
unless it's dark night everyone in bed
Other sounds are creak of chair & floor, water
dripping on heater from laundry, cat licking itself
   & occasional peck on typewriter, peck on my cheek

Unless it's dark night everyone in bed
   I'm wide awake hungry wet lonely thinking
occasional peck on typewriter, peck on my cheek
   My brain cells grow, I get bigger

I'm wide awake wet lonely hungry thinking
Then Mamma pulls out breast, says "Milky?"
My brain cells grow, I get bigger
   This is my first Christmas in the world

Mamma pulls out breast, says "Milky?"
   Daddy conducts a walking tour of house
This is my first Christmas in the world
   I study knots in pine wood ceiling

Daddy conducts a walking tour of house
I study pictures of The Madonna del Parto, a
   sweet-faced Buddha & Papago Indian girl
I study knots in pine wood ceiling
   I like contrasts, stripes, eyes & hairlines

I study pictures of The Madonna del Parto, a
sweet-faced Buddha & Papago Indian girl
   Life is colors, faces are moving
I like contrasts, stripes, eyes & hairlines
   I don't know what I look like

Life is colors, faces are moving
   They love me smiling
I don't know what I look like
   I try to speak of baby joys & pains

They love me smiling
   She takes me through a door, the wind howls
I try to speak of baby joys & pains
   I'm squinting, light cuts through my skin

She takes me through a door, the wind howls
   Furry shapes & large vehicles move close
I'm squinting, light cuts through my skin
   World is vast I'm in it with closed eyes

I rest between her breasts, she places me on dry leaves
  He carries me gently on his chest & shoulder
I'm locked in little dream, my fists are tight
  They showed me moon in sky, was something
in my dream

He carries me gently on his chest & shoulder
  He calls me sweet baby, good baby boy
They showed me moon in sky, was something
in my dream
  She is moving quickly & dropping things

He calls me sweet baby, good baby boy
  She sings hush go to sleep right now
She is moving quickly & dropping things
  They rock my cradle, they hold me tightly in their arms

She sings hush go to sleep right now
  She wears red nightgown, smells of spice & milk
They rock my cradle, they hold me tightly in their arms
  I don't know any of these words or things yet

She wears a red nightgown, smells of spice & milk
  He has something woolen and rough on
I don't know any of these words or things yet
  I sit in my chair & watch what moves

He has something woolen & rough on
  I can stretch & unfold as he holds me in the bath
I sit in my chair & watch what moves
  I see when things are static or they dance

I can stretch & unfold as he holds me in the bath
  Water is soft I came from water
I can see when things are static or they dance
  like flames, the cat pouncing, shadows or light
  streaming in

Water is soft I came from water
    Not that long ago I was inside her
like flames, the cat pouncing, shadows or light
streaming in
    I heard her voice then I remember now

Not that long ago I was inside her
    I lie in my crib midday this is
always changing, I am expanding toward you
    Mamma's sweeping or else boiling water for tea.

MARILYN NELSON WANIEK
SENSE OF DISCOVERY

Frankly, I find it easier to write in form than to write in free verse. There's a sense of closure, of completeness, in form which doesn't exist in free verse, and a tremendous sense of discovery in finding a rhyme or slant-rhyme. For slant-rhyme, I find that if I listen to the "weight" of the vowels, then balanced vowel sounds of equivalent "weights," the poem... I don't know how to say this... feels satisfying. The use of form seems to me to be more appropriate for poems about the historical past, and the rhythmical, "dancy" music for the poem about a dance ("Diverne's Waltz") seems... well, it just feels right. As for the sonnets: I've been experimenting with sonnets for some time, and enjoy working within that small tight space. I do not especially advocate formalist verse, though it does, I think, offer more "memorability" than free verse, and a strong sense of being part of a long tradition.

DIVERNE'S WALTZ

Diverne stands in the kitchen as they dance,
laughing and flirting, on the bare parlor floor.
She's taken up the rug, glad for the chance,
at last, to beat it free of sins outdoors.

Her fancy cakes are popular, her punch
has earned light giggles from Miss Atwood's friends.
She'd struggled at Miss Atwood's back to cinch
that tiny waist. *Miss Atwood look right grand.*

Mister Tyler asks for a water-glass of rye:
he's just enlisted, a drop-out from law school.
She notices something dangerous in his eye:
Crazy damn white man, acting like a fool.

Taking her hands, Henry Tyler gives her a twirl
and off they waltz. He swirls Diverne so fast
her head kerchief unknots itself. He smiles
down at Diverne's embarrassment, and gasps:

They blush! Hearing the whispers from the walls,
he sees men grin. His father shakes his head.
But *(That dark rose...)* he dances. *What the hell,
who knows? next week, next month, I could be dead.*

CHOSEN

Diverne wanted to die, that August night
his face hung over hers, a sweating moon.
She wished so hard, she killed part of her heart.

If she had died, her one begotten son,
her life's one light, would never have been born.
Pomp Atwood might have been another man:

born with a single race, another name.
Diverne might not have known the starburst joy
her son would give her. And the man who came

out of a twleve-room house and ran to her
close shack across three yards that night, to leap
onto her cornshuck pallet. Pomp was their

share of the future. And it wasn't rape.
In spite of her raw terror. And his whip.

BALANCE

He watch her like a coonhound watch a tree.
What might explain the metamorphosis
he underwent when she paraded by
with tea-cakes, in her fresh and shabby dress?
(As one would carry water from a well—
straight-backed, high-headed, like a diadem,
with careful grace so that no drop will spill—
she balanced, almost brimming, her one name.)

She think she something, stuck-up island bitch.
Chopping wood, hanging laundry on the line,
and tantalizingly within his reach,
she honed his body's yearning to a keen,
sharp point. And on that point she balanced life.
That hoe Diverne think she Marse Tyler's wife.

DAUGHTERS, 1900

Five daughters, in the slant light on the porch,
are bickering. The eldest has come home
with new truths she can hardly wait to teach.

She lectures them: the younger daughters search
the sky, elbow each others' ribs, and groan.
Five daughters, in the slant light on the porch

and blue-sprigged dresses, like a stand of birch
saplings whose leaves are going yellow-brown
with new truths. They can hardly wait to teach,

themselves, to be called "Ma'am," to march
high-heeled across the hanging bridge to town.
Five daughters. In the slant light on the porch

Pomp lowers his paper for a while, to watch
the beauties he's begotten with his Ann:
these new truths they can hardly wait to teach.

The eldest sniffs, "A lady doesn't scratch."
The third snorts back, "Knock, knock: nobody home."
The fourth concedes, "Well, maybe not in *church*..."
Five daughters in the slant light on the porch.

THE BALLAD OF AUNT GENEVA

Geneva was the wild one.
Geneva was a tart.
Geneva met a blue-eyed boy
and gave away her heart.

Geneva ran a roadhouse.
Geneva wasn't sent
to college like the others:
Pomp's pride her punishment.

She cooked out on the river,
watching the shore slide by,
her lips pursed into hardness,
her deep-set brown eyes dry.

They say she killed a woman
over a good black man
by braining the jealous heifer
with an iron frying pan.

They say, when she was eighty,
she got up late at night
and sneaked her old, white lover in
to make love, and to fight.

First, they heard the tell-tale
singing of the springs,

then Geneva's voice rang out:
I need to buy some things,

So next time, bring more money.
And bring more moxie, too.
I ain't got no time to waste
on limp white mens like you.

Oh yeah? Well, Mister White Man,
it sure might be stone-white,
but my thing's white as it is.
And you know damn well I'm right.

Now listen: take your heart pills
and pay the doctor mind.
If you wake up and die on me,
I'll whip your white behind.

They tiptoed through the parlor
on heavy, time-slowed feet.
She watched him, from her front door,
walk down the dawnlit street.

Geneva was the wild one.
Geneva was a tart.
Geneva met a blue-eyed boy
and gave away her heart.

A CANTICLE FOR ABBA JACOB

1.

How beautiful you are, my love,
how beautiful you are. I always knew
you were a redwood in a grove
of mangoes: shadows under you
fragranced, cool as an Easter morning's dew.

2.

Twelve thousand miles. He sees me first,
and calls me. And his eyes are just the same.
I don't know which of these is worse:
the joy of turning toward my name,
or the pain of smothering a rising flame.

3.

He talks about a helpless God;
walking with me, he holds up his white hem.
He listens, smiles, and nods. The God
of the Desert Fathers' apothegms,
who seeks the poor, who lights our world through them.

4.

At lunch in the refectory
he feeds me from a papaya with his spoon.
Joy curves in a trajectory
which I visualize as a cartoon
of a contrail fading miles beyond the moon.

5.

A paring knife slices my thumb.
He jumps up, takes the bandage from my hand,
and binds it. I feel, yielding, dumb,
his tenderness and his command.
His dark hair.... We step back. We understand.

6.

The territory-marking calls
of morning birds divide darkness from day.
Within white oratory walls
a hermit and a mother pray.
They pray in silence. God knows what they say.

7.

Ad te clamamus exsules...

How perfectly plainsong's twin poles combine
to raise the soul's lamenting praise,
its joyous heart-break.
                              I incline
my head and chant: Beloved, I am Thine.

8.

My Love is coming toward my room,
Like Cinderella on her wedding night,
who waits, breathing her own perfume,
I tremble, heartsick with delight.
The Bridegroom comes. His gentle eyes. His might.

9.

I sleep, but my night-watching heart
hears my Beloved calling through the door.
I run to force steel bars apart
and open to Him. But before
I breathe free air, He's not there anymore.

10.

I seek Him on my bed whom my
heart loves. Impossible. I cannot find
a trace under the curving sky.
And still I cannot stop my mind
searching for Him who left my heart behind.

11.

How beautiful You are, my Love,
how beautiful You are.
                Your changeful eyes,
the humble grace with which you move
your hands, your laughter, your surprise.
Your listening silences. Your God, who dies.

12.

He nestles me in His embrace.
Don't rouse my Love. My breath mingles with His.

The quiet contours of his face:
Touch them as I would. I pray this.
Touch him for me, my Lord.
                My Love! Thy kiss!

KATHLEENE WEST
E.B. AND ME

Almost anything I say about form has to include that long-ago semester I studied with Elizabeth Bishop, visiting poet at the University of Washington in 1974. I remember with disturbing clarity her informing me that in my first poem in assigned abab rhyme scheme, I had failed to achieve correct rhyme, that my end word "milking" was not a full rhyme with "spring"; that it called for a word like "bilking." The idea of such an incongruous word in my stiff little pastoral troubled me, and I stuffed the poem into the back of my notebook, hoping I'd impress her with my verbal dexterity in later assignments. A few poems later, with the villanelle, Bishop had to point out to me that "dream" and "seen" were not exact rhymes, that in fact she felt the "rhyming" of the "m" and "n" consonants the most grating sound in the English language. I don't remember being mortified, although I'm sure I was. I do remember both incidents opening an awareness of the, for me, completely untouched realm of modern poetry written in form. I thought formal verse meant sonnets. Now there were villanelles, sestinas, and with Babette Deutsch's marvelous *Poetry Handbook*, triolets, roundels, and innumerable others. There was also the novel idea of other kinds of rhyme besides "perfect rhyme." I began to notice poets from all centuries making use of half rhymes, slant-rhymes, and I realized how well Bishop had taught me, using the stance of the "purist."

I used to have a bad habit of saving anything new, hoarding the shirt, the towels, even the pad of paper for some indeterminate time in the future when it would be proper to use these stored-up articles. I'm a bit that way with forms, waiting until I think my poetry needs a strong imaginative lift that I can't seem to get from words and ideas alone, or until a difficult experience comes along that I need to make sense of in verse. Then, that same sense of discovery I felt sixteen years ago comes back. My own language will surprise me. I will write what I didn't know I needed to say. This has always been one of the prime purposes of poetry, to write, as Sam Hamill used to say, "to find out what's on my mind." Writing with a predetermined shape is one way I can find out.

ON TRACK

Say happiness is possible, or more than possible,
Available for those who hold the key belief,
Satisfy ancestors, cast the proper spell,
Compliment all the gods, eat complementary proteins,
Exercise the heart to maintain aerobic emotion,
Promise to shun abstractions down to the last detail.
Details distract me, I'm charmed by singularities—
    Where are they going—those beautiful young men
      on the train?

City of New Orleans, the Zephyr, British Rail—
Real trains, imagined excursions, carry me
Probing for love and work with wearisome zeal.
Pleasures accrue with fewer touches of irony:
Choices unashamed, unexplained to a baleful UC:
Moon-rise in a desert, a country after revolution,
A chance to meditate on certain scenery—
    Where are they going—those beautiful young men
      on the train?

One on to Denver; another left at Cedar Falls.
Elsewhere they live, like famous folk or deities.
And like the Voice in the burning bush, the Kennedy
 at the mall,
Leaving, they give a piquant fulfillment—and relief.
Dubious, the best-learned lesson, the strongest
 pleasure bittersweet.
Still, I want it all, to mingle thought and sensation.
Let metaphor guide me on literal journies—
 Where are they going—those beautiful young men
  on the train?

Muses Adoniac, I praise your temporal glory,
Inspiration waiting, as always, at the next station,
With strong, shy arms, ambition, and nearly perfect teeth,
Gracing us briefly, you beautiful young men on the train.

* UC—"unwilling companion," Martha Gellhorn's descrip-
tion of Ernest Hemingway on a 1941 "nightmare visit to
China."

MILDRED WESTON
To Be Clearly Heard

My use of "formal verse" has covered forty years—
because it comes naturally to me, and because I be-
lieve in form as having a beginning, middle, and end,
with sound and sense and clarity. Sometimes I write
in strict rhyme and meter, other times relaxed some-
what—but still to be clearly heard.

PRIMITIVE PLACE

Somewhere under sand
my ancient cities lie.
Their columns left behind
were given to the wind,
to withering desert sun,
to earthquake or to flood—
such tides as cover over
the site where temples stood.

Through ages laid in layers,
from shards the diggers know
the greatest of my structures
fell deeper still below;
beyond the reach of labor
where time and tools are lost
with undiscovered ruins
in rock and waste and salt.

DEPARTURE

Down the dim aisle of standing pullman coaches
blurred in the grey dust-powdered light,
I tilt my shoulders to the weight I carry
across this night.

Away from mingled voices in the station,
on time and guided as the ticket shows,
I am instructed so myself may follow
the track I chose.

Revolving thought begins with steady motion
to wind its circles round an iron core.
The private pulse identifies with power
as conquerer.

I take my leave of stationary places.
My resting place shall be a moving berth
where slow foosteps give over to the paces
that claim the earth.

GAIL WHITE
BEING HUMAN

In spite of decaades of free verse ascendency, I still think of formal verse as "real poetry." I grew up on the great English poets, I like to think of myself in the tradition of Yeats, Byron, and Donne. I regard the trend back to formal verse which has sprung up in recent years as one of the few hopeful signs that the fine arts have not yet perished.

For what it's worth, I also like the nineteenth-century novel, representational painting, and sculptures that bear a resemblance, still recognizable, to the human body. Because when we've exhausted the world as our senses perceive it, we've exhausted the possibilities of being human.

THE LEOPARD IN EDEN

Those two are gone who walked upright on two legs
with hair on head and shoulders and nowhere else,
gone with their scent of cultivated flowers
and crude variations on our innocence.

The dark now glistens only with our eyes,
the purr and prowl of our voices. From our fur
the rain falls like soft hands—they could not stroke
our heads without a prescience of terror...

And gone at last they are, contriving shelters
of wood and stone and second skins of leaves,
because they had no decent lust to kill
but a base instinct to cheat and to deceive.

CAROLYN BEARD WHITLOW
Standards to Break

Poetry in form demands a formal conformity, a commitment to the making of a definitive, defineable, nameable artifact. I like the notion that a predetermined shape, size, color, depth, breadth, veneer all harness that definition. I like the mathematics of formal poetry, its algebra, its challenges, its "rightness" or "wrongness," its rules, standards to meet, match, exceed, break—the "break" for me most often in the poem's subject matter: to air— in this context of elegance—the nation's dirty underwear.

BOOK OF ROUTH

I learn to live by guile, to do without love.
I'm not scared. I wait in the dark for you,
Sleeping to avoid death, tired of sleep.
 The withered dyed rug fades, dims, fades, recolors,
 Warp frayed, weft unraveled; as light looms dark,
I doubt I'm happy as can be in this house.

Outside no one would guess inside this house
I learn to live by guise, disguise my pain. Love
Dinner served by pyre light, sit doused by dark,
 Cornered in my room, wait in the dark for you.
 The bureau melts to shadow; that unraveled,
  uncolors.
Sleep to avoid death, tired of sleep,

 I avoid the mirror, the lie of truth. You sleep
Downstairs, chin lobbed over, chair rocked, spilled,
 house

Distilled in techtonic dreams of technicolor,
   Mostly golf course green and Triumph blue. I love
   Earthpots, cattails, a fireplace, no reflection of you.
While you sleep, I sip steeped ceremonial teas, dark

   As coffee, your swirled wineglass breathing dark
Downstairs fumes in the living dead room. Sleep
Comes easy, comes easy. I'm not scared. For you
   I curtsy before your mother, say I love this house.
   I love this house, this room. I love this. I love.
The traffic light blinks black and white. No color.

   Come Monday, I'll dustmop, repaper with multicolor
Prints, zigzag zebra stripe rooms, fuschias, no dark
Blue or sober gray, none of the colors that you love.
   Insomnia is sweet, I think, the once I cannot sleep:
   I'm not scared. I'm not scared. This is my house.
Illumined by darkness, I watch my dark mirror you.

   No. No silent hostage to the dark, I know you
Cast a giant shadow in a grim fairy tale, colors
Bloodlet, blueblack, spineless yellow trim this house;
   Escaped maroon, I emerge from a chrysalined dark,
   Succumb, mesmered under a light spring-fed sleep,
Nightmare over, giddy, without sleep, with love.

   The colors of the room fade into dust, house now dark.
I'm not scared. I learn to live without you, with love,
   To do without sleeping to avoid death, tired of sleep.

ROCKIN' A MAN, STONE BLIND

Cake in the oven, clothes out on the line,
Night wind blowin' against sweet, yellow thighs,
Two-eyed woman rockin' a man stone blind.

Man smell of honey, dark like coffee grind;
Countin' on his fingers since last July.
Cake in the oven, clothes out on the line.

Mister Jacobs say he be colorblind,
But got to tighten belts and loosen ties.
Two-eyed woman rockin' a man stone blind.

Winter becoming angry, rent behind.
Strapping spring sun needed to make mud pies.
Cake in the oven, clothes out on the line.

Looked in the mirror, Bessie's face I find.
I be so down low, my man be so high.
Two-eyed woman rockin' a man stone blind.

Policemans found him; damn near lost my mind.
Can't afford no flowers; can't even cry.
Cake in the oven, clothes out on the line.
Two-eyed woman rockin' a man stone blind.

POEM FOR THE CHILDREN

take your first steps in a Walker,
   come on out of your Yarde.
      Cruse the Jordan river,
         ride the Redding railroad,

catch a Coltrane.
   soar on a Scott-Heron—
      I mean fly like a Byrd.
         stroll for Miles through a Woodson,

talk to the trees;
   bring me a Bunche of flowers:
      pick me a Rosa in the Parks;
     bathe in a Tubman

so you can babble like a Brooks.
   know the ABC's through
      Malcolm X, letters like W.E.B.
     Seale me an envelope,

mail it with a Stampp.
   Marshall all your strength;
     strive to know the Truth.
       introduce yourself to Lincoln,

shake hands with Booker T.
   learn for every wrong
     there's a Wright,
       and I'll crown you like a King.

NANCY WILLARD
The Gift of a Poem

I suppose my love of formal poetry goes back to my love of music and children's games: the folk songs and the skipping rope rhymes I learned as a child. In graduate school, I did a lot of work on medieval carols and refrains. Sometimes form gives you the poem. When I was trying to find the right voice and form to use in *The Ballad of Biddy Early*, I went back to Irish ballads and Gaelic charms.

THE BALLAD OF BIDDY EARLY

"I've an empty stomach,
you've an empty purse.
You feel your fingers freezing?
Outside it's ten times worse,
so listen to my story.
Forget the wind and rain.
It's time for bed," the tinker said,
"but pass the cup again.

"I sing of Biddy Early,
the wise woman of Clare.
Many's the man admires her
carrot-colored hair,
and many those that come to her
on horseback or by cart,
for she can heal a broken leg
or a broken heart.

"She keeps a magic bottle
in whose majestic eye
a tiny coffin twinkles
and if it sinks, you die.
It rises, you grow better
and slip out of your pain.
It's time for bed," the tinker said,
"but pass the cup again.

"She covers the great bottle
and runs to fetch the small,
filled with a bright elixir,
honey and sage and gall.
She'll take no gold or silver
but maybe a speckled hen.
It's time for bed," the tinker said,
"Let's pass the cup again.

"*Follow the stream*, she told me.
Go where the salmon goes.
Avoid mischievous bridges
for even water knows
if you should drop this bottle—"
He turned and spoke no more.
Biddy Early's shadow
was listening at the door.

THE CAT'S SECOND SONG

There was an old woman of Clare
who was often seen riding a bear.
It ate candles and hay
till it twinkled away
down a tunnel of emerald air.

THE SPECKLED HEN'S MORNING SONG TO BIDDY EARLY

Let the speckled hens praise her.
Let the nine nations of slugs honor her.
Let the ten tribes of sparrows rejoice in her:

High-stepper, moon-catcher,
keeper of starlight in dark jars,
protector of pigs, saver of spiders.

Praise her from whom all cracked corn flows,
for whom the stars go willingly to roost,
for whom the gold loaf in the sky rises.

262

NELLIE WONG
WHEN FORM FLOWERS

When I first became interested in poetry in the 1970's, I turned to reading English translations of haiku and tanka, the Japanese forms, because they fascinated me. I was intrigued by the imagery, the density and light that shone from the pages of the books I was reading. A scene of nature was usually evoked in the poems I read, so I began to think of writing some short poems, realizing that the haiku form was limiting, yet freeing. I tried my hand at writing some haiku, not clearly understanding why this form flowered, why the images came from my heart and my hands. I believed then—and I still do—that there was a symbiotic relationship between the words and me, between the haiku form and the world I lived in. How tantalized I was to envision birds flying against the sky as words took off from my pen onto the page.

I began a love affair with making form. At the same time I realized that form alone wasn't what intrigued me. The colors, textures, shapes and sounds of words fell onto the page, forming a collage, a content, that held me in awe. Indeed, I discovered magic in making form, but I loved the content of the poem as well. I discovered the power of words, not loose beads lying unused in a sewing basket, but strung into a necklace that could be worn.

I like using form to see what I can come up with—something new, something different. Sometimes I'll use a line of someone else's poem and see what words flow onto the page. Sometimes I'll put letters of my name down vertically on the left-hand margin of a page and make a new poem, restricted by the necessity of writing down a word that must begin with a specific letter that is already on the page. I'm unable to choose a word of my own. Yet, at the same time, I am choosing a different word compelled by a certain letter of the alphabet.

In Bertolt Brecht's poem, "Praise of Learning," the poet writes:

> Learn the ABC. It won't be enough,
> but learn it! Don't be dismayed by it!
> Begin! You must know everything.
> You must take over the leadership.

Writing poetry, making whole from form and content, is learning the ABC. I am enthralled by it. I, along with my comrades and co-workers, must know everything. We must take over the leadership.

IRONING

Papa drank and ate
while I ironed my family's clothes.
In our silence he blurts:
"Marriage, hmphh!"
I did not answer Papa's words.
I only ironed my family's clothes.

GRANDMOTHERS' SONG

Grandmothers sing their song
Blinded by the sun's rays
Grandchildren for whom they long
For pomelo-golden days

Blinded by the sun's rays
Gold bracelets, opal rings
For pomelo-golden days
Tiny fingers, ancient things

Gold bracelets, opal rings
Sprinkled with Peking dust
tiny fingers, ancient things
So young they'll never rust

Sprinkled with Peking dust
To dance in fields of mud
So young they'll never rust
Proud as if of royal blood

To dance in fields of mud
or peel shrimp for pennies a day
Proud as if of royal blood
Coins and jade to put away

Or peel shrimp for pennies a day
Seaweed washes up the shore
Coins and jade to put away
A camphor chest is home no more

Seaweed washes up the shore
bound feet struggle to loosen free
A camphor chest is home no more
A foreign tongue is learned at three

Bound feet struggle to loosen free
Grandchildren for whom they long
A foreign tongue is learned at three
Grandmothers sing their song

CELESTE TURNER WRIGHT
My Experience with Poetic Forms

Born in 1906, granted a Ph.D. in 1928, I have felt at home with traditional forms of verse. My mother wrote poems and delighted me by reciting a long rhymed poem (not her own) on the subject of Mary, Queen of Scots. Mother's copy of *Hiawatha* further enhanced my love of narrative verse. At my schoolhouse in the pines of Maine, where I toiled to keep up with my two older classmates, I sighed over a dead sweetheart of Whittier's, a lost infant daughter of James Russell Lowell's.

After moving to California in my teens, I published sonnets in the Pasadena *Star-News*. I chose sonnets as an exciting challenge and tried to obey the strictest rules of the form. As Stevenson said about writing *Treasure Island*, "it was awful fun!" I preferred sonnets to bridge or crossword puzzles. Later on, two famous poet-friends advised me not to write love-sonnets—"who can compete with Petrarch or Shakespeare?" And one poet added, "Leave out the damned literary allusions!" It was hard to be myself.

It was also hard to find a magazine that would print sonnets. Like a female Van Winkle, I woke up to find the poetry world changed. None of the well-known magazines wanted sonnets. Finally, as a life-saver, Josephine Miles gave me a list of little magazines—for example, *The Lyric*—which still liked traditional forms. Now there are more magazines that publish formal verse, like *The Formalist*—to which, of course, I enthusiastically subscribe.

STATE OF PRESERVATION

When Cromwell "slighted" Kenilworth,
The chapels, being shoddy, fell;
He bared the kitchens deep in earth
And left the banquet-hall a shell.

Only a graceful window-sheath
Recalls how Leicester loved to take
His wine with great Elizabeth;
The castle's cut like wedding-cake.

Far to the north at Linlithgow
The palace floors are winterworn,
The naked hearths are piled with snow,
Where once a royal girl was born.

Power and vengefulness prevail,
And yet at Warwick I have seen
A handkerchief, at Wilton pale
Hair that belonged to England's queen.

Fire and time relentlessly
Burn, yet at Holyrood I found
A basket for embroidery—
The silken skeins that Mary wound.

Appendixes

APPENDIX 1:
FORMAL KEY TO POEMS

ELIZABETH ALEXANDER

"Kevin of the N.E. Crew": Folk stanza. The heavily accentual, often falling rhythm evokes the form's history in oral poetry. Basically a long folk stanza (four beats per line), expressively altered in the third and last stanza.

"Ladders": Basically a three-beat accentual quatrain rhymed (axax).

"Who I Think You Are": Sicilian quatrains (abba) with at least one falling rhyme in each stanza, adding to the nursery-rhyme-like trochaic effect, though several of the lines are iambic.

"Zodiac": Unrhymed quatrains, iambic pentameter except for a trochaic and a dactylic line for emphasis in the second stanza (lines 3 and 4). A headless iambic pentameter (line 3) in the last stanza picks up on the falling rhythm of those two lines, keeping the rhythm within the meter as the blossoms remain within the tree.

NELL ALTIZER

"Sonnet 2" and "Sonnet 5" (from "Love Letters Written to Her Who Lives [Alas!] Away"): Petrarchan sonnets with an unusual rhyme scheme: English rhymes (abab) in the octave and a sestet rhyming (efgegf). The rhymes are also irregular, often slightly off or forced, and the meter, usually recognizable as iambic pentameter, has non-metrical passages such as the end of line 5 of the first sonnet, with its two trochees, or the last four lines of the second sonnet.

Julia Alvarez

"How I Learned to Sweep": Mostly iambic tetrameter couplets, with many initial trochees.

"Naming the Fabrics": Four-beat accentual quatrains rhymed (aabb).

"Sonnet 1" and "Sonnet 42" (from "33"): Metrically irregular Shakespearean sonnets, hovering around iambic pentameter but never staying with it.

"Bilingual Sestina": Non-metrical sestina with occasional lines of iambic pentameter.

Judith Barrington

"Villanelle VI": Villanelle. Four-beat and five-beat accentual lines with a strong anapestic swing; several lines are in iambic pentameter.

Rosellen Brown

"Five Poems from *Cora Fry*": Syllabics.

Debra Bruce

"Two Couples": Iambic tetrameter rhymed (ababcdcd) etc. (with many off-rhymes), changing to (aabbc) to close the poem.

"Sonnet 2" and "Sonnet 4" (from "The Light They Make"): Shakespearean sonnets, with several slant-rhymes.

Julia Budenz

"Poeta Fui": Petrarchan sonnet.

Melissa Cannon

"The Sisters": Petrarchan sonnet with an irregularly rhymed sestet (efgfef).

KELLY CHERRY

"History": Shakespearean sonnet.

"The Raiment We Put On": Shakespearean sonnet.

"The Bride of Quietness": English quatrains in iambic pentameter.

"Reading, Dreaming, Hiding": A nonce form based on the simple repetition of words.

"The Pines Without Peer": Two-beat accentual couplets.

SANDRA CISNEROS

"Muddy Kid Comes Home": Two-beat accentual line.

"The Poet Reflects on Her Solitary Fate": Two-beat accentual lines with slant-rhyme in second stanza and an extra line inserted in third stanza.

CHERYL CLARKE

"What Goes Around Comes Around, or The Proof is in the Pudding": Non-metrical villanelle.

"Tortoise and Badger": Non-metrical Shakespearean sonnet.

"Rondeau": Non-metrical rondeau.

CATHERINE DAVIS

"Belongings": Blank verse.

"The Years": Iambic trimeter rhymed (ababxx).

"Out of Work, Out of Touch, Out of Sorts": Iambic trimeter rhymed (abacbdcdfgfe) (an original rhyme scheme), with many trochaic substitutions.

RITA DOVE

"Persephone Underground": Non-metrical sonnet, with a reversed Shakespearean rhyme scheme that starts with the couplet.

"History": Non-metrical sonnet, with nonce rhyme scheme based on a reversed Shakespearean sonnet.

Rita Dove (con't.)

"Political": Non-metrical sonnet with octave and sestet divisions based on the Petrarchan sonnet, but a nonce rhyme scheme.

"'Blown apart by loss...'": Non-metrical sonnet with nonce rhyme scheme.

Suzanne J. Doyle

"This Shade": Iambic pentameter English quatrains, with falling rhyme in third stanza.

"Some Girls": Iambic pentameter rhymed (abab), with concluding iambic hexameter.

"Hell to Pay": Heroic couplets.

Rhina P. Espaillat

"Metrics": Iambic Italian quatrains, with a different pattern of line lengths in each stanza (5-4-4-5, 5-5-5-2, 5-5-5-2).

Julie Fay

"Dear Marilyn": Slant-rhyming English quatrains, some rhyming (xaxa). Meter hovers loosely around four-beat or five-beat lines, with occasional iambic pentameters.

"Words": Rhymed triplets, with the three-syllable rhyme words echoing the triple rhymes within stanzas and also echoing the frequent three-syllable rhymes of Italian poetry.

Annie Finch

"Dickinson": Half-stanzas of common meter (a hymn stanza alternating iambic tetrameters and trimeters), with the last line of each stanza slant-rhyming with the other last lines.

"For Grizzel McNaught (1709–1792)": Terza rima in iambic tetrameter.

"A Reply from His Coy Mistress": Iambic tetrameter couplets, as in the poem by Andrew Marvell to which this one replies.

"Sapphics for Patience": Sapphic stanzas.

Joan Austin Geier

"On Your Twenty-First Birthday": Rhyme royal, roughly in iambic pentameter, but with some tetrameters and some irregular or non-metrical lines.

Sarah Gorham

"The White Tiger Leaps," "Princess Parade," and "The Empress Receives the Head of a Taiping Rebel": Non-metrical Shakespearean sonnets, with regular rhyme pattern but many slant-rhymes and eye rhymes.

Jane Greer

"Rodin's 'Gates of Hell'": Iambic tetrameter rhymed (ababcdcd) etc.

Emily Grosholz

"Eden": Five-line stanzas of iambic pentameter, with the third and fifth lines slant-rhymed.

"The Last of the Courtyard": Villanelle, with variations in repeating lines, iambic pentameter.

"Legacies": Ten-line unrhymed stanzas of iambic pentameter, with one line of iambic trimeter in each stanza, and a number of headless lines counteracting the forward movement.

Marilyn Hacker

"Eight Days in April": Crown of sonnets.

"Ballad of Ladies Lost and Found": Ballade stanza, modified to rhyme (abbaaabbacC), with C being the refrain.

"Dusk: July": Sapphics.

Rachel Hadas

"The House Beside the Sea": Loosely linked refrains, meter usually iambic, with many iambic pentameters.

"Winged Words": A nine-line stanza that suggests the rhyme scheme of the Spenserian stanza, but uses four rhyme-sounds instead of three. Primarily iambic tetrameter, with an occasional strong triple rhythm, particularly in the seventh stanza. The last stanza consists of the final lines of all previous stanzas.

"The Lair": Irregularly rhyming tercets; two lines of iambic trimeter and the rest iambic pentameter, occasionally headless or missing the last stress.

Josephine Jacobsen

"Only Alice": Quatrains rhymed (abab), of varying iambic line lengths.

"The Limbo Dancer": Sestina, altering the expected pattern of repeating words in several places, and using parts of words as end-words with unusual freedom. Iambic pentameter (except for the fourth line from the end), with free use of spondees, anapests, and the rest or missed syllable at the caesura.

Lenore Keeshig-Tobias

"I Grew Up": Two repeating patterns: the italicized refrain and the initial stanza which then concludes the last section.

"Mother With Child": Repeated elements directly follow each other.

Dolores Kendrick

"Solo: The Good Blues": Basically three-beat accentual line, with refrain.

"Note to the Opthalmologist": Non-metrical quatrains rhyming (axax).

"Gethsemane A.D.": Quatrains rhymed (abab), varying from three to four accents per line, with two lines of iambic pentameter in last stanza.

"We Are the Writing on the Wall": Non-metrical tercets rhyming with each other in their final lines.

JANE KENYON:

"Travel: After a Death": Blank verse.

"Inpatient": Blank verse.

"Alone for a Week": Iambic trimeter.

MARY KINZIE

"Sun and Moon": Sapphic stanzas.

"Boy": Rhyme royal, with a short line for emphasis in the third stanza.

"Sound Waves": Ballade.

"Canicula": Eight haiku.

"Ringing Words": Blank verse.

CAROLYN KIZER

"On a Line from Valéry": Villanelle, iambic pentameter, with variations in repeated lines.

"Section Two" and "Section Three" (from "Pro Femina"): Five-beat to six-beat, often strongly dactylic lines, often with a final trochee. This meter echoes the classical epic meter, dactylic hexameter. Iambic pentameter at the end of "Section 2."

"A Muse of Water": Unrhymed iambic tetrameter.

PHYLLIS KOESTENBAUM

"Sonnet XXXVII from 'Criminal Sonnets'": Non-metrical Shakespearean sonnet, loosely slant-rhymed, though lacking the second rhyme in the third tercet.

SYBIL KOLLAR

"Sunday Matinee": Shakespearean sonnet, based in iambic pentameter but occasionally non-metrical as in lines 2, 3, and 6.

SYBIL KOLLAR (CON'T.)

"Late Arrivals": Shakespearean sonnet, iambic pentameter except for the first quatrain, which has a four-beat accentual rhythm.

MAXINE KUMIN

"The Height of the Season": Five-beat accentual verse, with a triple-rhythm undercurrent.

"The Nuns of Childhood: Two Views": Double villanelle, triple-foot tetrameter rhythm.

"Despair": Petrarchan sonnet, with many anapestic substitutions.

PHILLIS LEVIN

"Citizens & Sky": Iambic pentameter quatrains, unrhymed.

"Dark Horse": Iambic tetrameter quatrains, slant-rhymed (abab).

"Planting Roses": Four-beat accentual quatrains, slant-rhymed (xaxa), varied in last stanza.

JANET LEWIS

"Time and Music": Iambic tetrameter quatrains rhymed (aabb).

VASSAR MILLER

"Light Reading": Shakespearean sonnet.

"How Far?": Common measure, with four beats in the last line instead of three for emphasis.

"Dirge in Jazz Time": Accentual rhythm with triple undercurrent, arranged as a ballad stanza followed by a four-beat couplet.

LESLIE MONSOUR

"Emily's Words": Heroic couplets.

"Sweeping": Nonce form (variation of terza rima).

"A Dream of Dying": Common measure.

HONOR MOORE

"First Time: 1950": Non-metrical sestina.

"A Green Place": Non-metrical sestina.

SUZANNE NOGUERE

"The Scribes": Sonnet.

"The Secret": Iambic pentameter (except for a line or two) rhymed (abab).

"Whirling Round the Sun": Sonnet.

"Soma": Ottava rima.

"Barney Bigard": Terza rima.

ELISE PASCHEN

"Litany": Iambic dimeter with many falling line endings.

"Confederacy": Anapestic dimeter.

MOLLY PEACOCK

"ChrisEaster": Non-metrical quatrains slant-rhymed (abab), with (aabb) for closure.

"Devolution": Roughly iambic pentameter, rhymed (ababcdcd) with a closing couplet.

"How I Had to Act": Decasyllabic lines, often iambic pentameter, arranged in tercets with two lines rhymed in each stanza.

"Anger Sweetened": Modified Shakespearean sonnet, non-metrical for first five lines, iambic pentameter thereafter.

"Good Girl": Variation on Shakespearean sonnet.

"The Spell": Pun-poem (nonce form).

HELEN PINKERTON

"On Dorothea Lange's Photograph 'Migrant Mother' (1936)": Blank verse.

"On Vermeer's 'Young Woman with a Water Jug' (1658) in the Metropolitan Museum": Blank verse, with a closing iambic hexameter.

MARY JO SALTER

"Chernobyl": Three-beat accentual quatrains rhymed (abab) with frequent falling rhyme.

"What Do Women Want?": Iambic pentameter with all lines rhymed, but irregularly.

"The Rebirth of Venus": English quatrains, iambic pentameter.

"Young Girl Peeling Apples": Roughly syllabic in the spiralling shape of an apple-peel, with varying rhyme patterns.

SONIA SANCHEZ

"Haiku (for paul robeson)": Haiku.

"Haiku": Haiku.

"Song No. 3": Blues form.

"Song No. 2": Chant with repetition (anaphora).

"Father and Daughter": Modified sonnet.

MAY SARTON

"Small Joys": Iambic pentameter, varying rhyme scheme.

"The Tortured": Common meter with a ballad stanza influence, resulting in a hybrid metric: four-beat accentual lines alternating with iambic trimeters.

MAUREEN SEATON

"Fear of Subways, " "Fear of Shoplifting," "Wings": Petrarchan sonnets (with some irregular rhymes), basically decasyllabic (especially the first two), but usually non-metrical.

LESLIE SIMON

"Hattie went to Market," "Nellie gives into Blanche," "Bernice got next to Isis": Free verse structured by consistent internal rhyme and simple repetition.

ELIZABETH SPIRES

"The Comb and the Mirror": Three-beat accentual line, irregularly rhymed.

"Apology": Two-beat accentual stanzas with repeated lines making a refrain.

"Interrogations of the Sparrow": Accentual ballad stanza with refrain.

MAURA STANTON

"Ballad of the Magic Glasses": Ballad stanza.

"Living Apart": Blank verse.

PATRICIA STORACE

"The Archaeology of Divorce": Iambic pentameter English quatrains, with many anapestic substitutions.

"Wedding Song": Nonce form based on accumulated repetition; iambic pentameter.

"King Lear Bewildered": Usually four-beat or five-beat accentual lines, irregular rhyme scheme.

MONA VAN DUYN

"Homework": Sicilian quatrains, iambic pentameter.

"The Vision Test": Iambic pentameter rhymed (abab), with a strong triple-rhythm undercurrent.

"Sonnet for Minimalists": Shakespearean sonnet in iambic dimeter.

ALMA LUZ VILLANUEVA

"Peace #3": Free verse, with anaphora.

"Even the Eagles Must Gather": Free verse, with anaphora and repetition.

Anne Waldman

"Baby's Pantoum": Pantoum, non-metrical.

Marilyn Nelson Waniek

"Diverne's Waltz": Quatrains, rhymed (abab), iambic pentameter.

"Chosen": Nonce form of sonnet, with tercets instead of quatrains followed by a couplet, iambic pentameter.

"Balance": Shakespearean sonnet.

"Daughters, 1900": Villanelle, iambic pentameter.

"The Ballad of Aunt Geneva": Ballad.

"A Canticle for Abba Jacob": Five-line stanzas consisting of an iambic tetrameter, an iambic pentameter, two more iambic tetrameters, and another iambic pentameter, rhymed (ababb).

Kathleene West

"On Track": Ballade, non-metrical, with a strong triple rhythm undercurrent.

Mildred Weston

"Primitive Place": Iambic trimeter rhymed (xaxa), with a strong trochaic undercurrent.

"Departure": Variable line length stanza with a strong falling rhythm (reminiscent of Sapphics).

Gail White

"The Leopard in Eden": Iambic pentameter quatrains, slant-rhymed (xaxa).

Carolyn Beard Whitlow

"Book of Routh": Sestina, iambic pentameter.

"Rockin' A Man, Stone Blind": Villanelle, five-beat accentual line.

"Poem for the Children": Pun-poem, (free verse).

NANCY WILLARD

"The Ballad of Biddy Early": Two folk stanzas in each stanza.

"The Cat's Second Song": Limerick.

"The Speckled Hen's Morning Song to Biddy Early": Chant with anaphora and parallelism.

NELLIE WONG

"Ironing": Simple repetition, accentual rhythm varying from two to four beats per line.

"Grandmothers' Song": Pantoum, non-metrical.

CELESTE TURNER WRIGHT

"State of Preservation": Iambic tetrameter quatrains rhymed (abab).

APPENDIX 2: INDEX OF FORMS

Note: Please see Appendix 1 (pg. 269) for more specific details on the form for each poem.

BALLAD:

BALLAD STANZA: See FOLK STANZA.

BALLADE:

BLANK VERSE:

BLUES FORM:

COMMON METER: See FOLK STANZA.

OTTAVA RIMA:

(pg. 168), "Soma," by Suzanne Noguere

PANTOUM:

(pg. 237), "Baby's Pantoum," by Anne Waldman
(pg. 263), "Grandmothers' Song," by Nellie Wong

PUN-POEMS:

(pg. 187), "The Spell," by Molly Peacock
(pg. 257), "Poem for the Children," by Carolyn B. Whitlow

QUATRAINS:

ENGLISH:

(pg. 11),   "Who I Think You Are," by Elizabeth Alexander
(pg. 41),   "The Bride of Quietness," by Kelly Cherry
(pg. 62),   "This Shade," by Suzanne J. Doyle
(pg. 65),   "Metrics," by Rhina P. Espaillat
(pg. 67),   "Dear Marilyn," by Julie Fay
(pg. 104), "Only Alice," by Josephine Jacobsen
(pg. 150), "Dark Horse," by Phillis Levin
(pg. 151), "Planting Roses," by Phillis Levin
(pg. 153), "Time and Music," by Janet Lewis
(pg. 182), "ChrisEaster," by Molly Peacock
(pg. 190), "Chernobyl," by Mary Jo Salter
(pg. 192), "The Rebirth of Venus," by Mary Jo Salter
(pg. 224), "The Archaeology of Divorce," by Patricia Storace
(pg. 241), "Diverne's Waltz," by Marilyn N. Waniek
(pg. 266), "State of Preservation," by Celeste T. Wright

ITALIAN:

(pg. 65),   "Metrics," by Rhina P. Espaillat
(pg. 115), "Gethsemane A.D.," by Dolores Kendrick
(pg. 228), "Homework," by Mona Van Duyn

OTHER RHYME SCEMES:

REPETITION:

ANAPHORA:

REFRAIN: See also BALLADE, VILLANELLE.

SIMPLE:

RHYME:

FALLING:
(pg. 11),   "Who I Think You Are," by Elizabeth Alexander
(pg. 154), "Light Reading," by Vassar Miller

IRREGULAR PATTERNS:
(pg. 191), "What Do Women Want?" by Mary Jo Salter
(pg. 193), "Young Girl Peeling Apples," by Mary Jo Salter
(pg. 202), "Small Joys," by May Sarton
(pg. 226), "King Lear Bewildered," by Patricia Storace ·

NONCE RHYME SCHEME:
(pg. 54),   "Out of Work, Out of Touch, Out of Sorts,"
            by Catherine Davis

SLANT-RHYME:
(pg. 14),   "Sonnet 2," by Nell Altizer
(pg. 15),   "Sonnet 5," by Nell Altizer
(pg. 67),   "Dear Marilyn," by Julie Fay
(pg. 70),   "Dickinson," by Annie Finch
(pg. 84),   "Eden," by Emily Grosholz
(pg. 139), "Sonnet XXXVII from 'Criminal Sonnets',"
            by Phyllis Koestenbaum
(pg. 205), "Fear of Subways," by Maureen Seaton
(pg. 206), "Fear of Shoplifting," by Maureen Seaton
(pg. 206), "Wings," by Maureen Seaton
(pg. 241), "Diverne's Waltz," by Marilyn N. Waniek
(pg. 254), "The Leopard in Eden," by Gail White

RHYME ROYAL:

(pg. 73),   "On Your Twenty-First Birthday,"
            by Joan Austin Geier
(pg. 125), "Boy," by Mary Kinzie

RONDEAU:

(pg. 50),   "Rondeau," [non-metrical] by Cheryl Clarke

CONTRIBUTORS' NOTES

ELIZABETH ALEXANDER
was born in New York City and grew up in Washington,
D.C. She received her B.A. from Yale University and her M.A.
from Boston University, where she studied with Derek Walcott.
Her poetry has appeared in many journals including *South-
ern Review* and *American Poetry Review*, and her first book,
The Venus Hottentot, was published in the Callaloo Poetry
Series in 1990. She is currently teaching at the University of
Chicago.

NELL ALTIZER'S
book of poems, *The Man Who Died En Route* (University of
Massachusetts Press, 1989) was the winner of the Juniper
Prize. Her poems have appeared in *13th Moon, Hawaii Re-
view, Massachusetts Review, Prairie Schooner*, and others. She
is currently Professor of English at the University of Ha-
waii, Honolulu.

JULIA ALVAREZ
was raised in the Dominican Republic and emigrated to the
United States in 1960. After receiving undergraduate and grad-
uate degrees in literature and writing, she taught poetry for
many years and published her first collection of poems, *Homecoming*,
in 1984. Alvarez has received grants from the National En-
dowment for the Arts and The Ingram Merrill Foundation.
Her novel *How the Garcia Girls Lost Their Accents* was the
winner of the 1991 PEN Oakland/Josephine Miles book award
for works which present a multicultural viewpoint. Alvarez
is currently professor of English at Middlebury College.

JUDITH BARRINGTON

is the author of two collections of poetry, *Trying to Be an Honest Woman* and most recently *History and Geography* (Eighth Mountain Press, 1989), which was a finalist for the Oregon Book Award, and an editor of *An Intimate Wilderness: Lesbian Writers on Sexuality*. In 1990, she was commissioned to write the libretto for an oratorio, *Mother of Us All* (music by David York), which was first performed in 1991. She is currently working on a book of memoirs about Spain.

ROSELLEN BROWN

is the author of four novels, including *Tender Mercies*, *Civil Wars*, and most recently *Before and After* (Dell, 1993); two collections of poetry; and a collection of short stories. Her work is also collected in *A Rosellen Brown Reader* (University Press of New England, 1992). She has published widely in magazines, won many awards including fellowships from the Guggenheim Foundation and the Bunting Institute, and was selected one of *Ms.* magazine's 12 "Women of the Year" in 1992. She teaches in the Creative Writing Program at the University of Houston.

DEBRA BRUCE

has published two books of poems, *Pure Daughter* and *Sudden Hunger* (Arkansas, 1987), which won the Carl Sandburg Literary Arts Award. In 1989 the sonnet sequence excerpted here, "The Light They Make," received the Gustav Davidson Memorial Award from the Poetry Society of America. She teaches in the English Department at Northeastern Illinois University.

JULIA BUDENZ

has an academic background in Greek, Latin, English, and comparative literature. Since about 1970 she has been writing a poem in five books, "The Gardens of Flora Baum," of which the conclusion of Book Two was published in 1984 by

Wesleyan University Press under the title *From the Gardens of Flora Baum*. The sonnet included in this anthology is taken from a sequence called "Sonnets to the Italian," which is a section of Book Three, "Rome," of the same long poem. Other sections and segments have appeared in American and British journals.

MELISSA CANNON

was born in New Hampshire and grew up in Tennessee. She is author of a chapbook, *Sister Fly Goes to Market*, and editor of the anthology of Tennessee writers *Homewords* (University of Tennessee Press, 1986). She lives in Nashville, where she works in the fast food industry.

KELLY CHERRY

has written four books of poetry, most recently *God's Loud Hand* (LSU Press, 1993). Her fifth novel, *My Life and Dr. Joyce Brothers* (Algonquin) appeared in 1990 and her first book of nonfiction, *The Exiled Heart* (LSU) in 1990. She has received the first Fellowship of Southern Writers Poetry Award, in recognition of a distinguished body of work.

SANDRA CISNEROS

was born in Chicago, the daughter of a Mexican father and a Mexican-Amercian mother. She is the author of *The House on Mango Street*, awarded the Before Columbus American Book Award in 1985, and *My Wicked Wicked Ways*. Her short story collection, *Woman Hollering Creek*, was published in 1991 and received the Lannan Award for Fiction, the PEN Center West Award for Fiction, the QPB New Voices in Fiction Award, and the Anisfield Wolf Award. Her work has been translated into seven languages. She has recently completed a new book of poetry, *Loose Woman*, and lives in San Antonio where she is at work on her novel, *Caramelo*.

CHERYL CLARKE

is the author of four books of poetry: *Narratives: Poems in the tradition of Black Women, Living as a Lesbian, Humid Pitch,* and most recently *experimental love* (Firebrand, 1993).

CATHERINE DAVIS

was born in 1924 in Minneapolis. She received her B.A. from George Washington University in 1961 and her M.A. from the University of Iowa Writers' Workshop in 1964. She also attended Stanford, the University of Chicago, and the University of Minnesota, and taught for many years, most recently as an instructor at the University of Massachusetts in Boston. Her poems have been published in many journals, including *Poetry, The New Yorker, Paris Review, Denver Quarterly, Iowa Review,* and the *North American Review.*

RITA DOVE

is the Poet Laureate of the United States for 1993-95. She received the 1987 Pulitzer Prize for her third book of poems, *Thomas and Beulah.* Other poetry books include *The Yellow House on the Corner, Museum, Grace Notes* (Norton) and most recently *Selected Poems* (Vintage, 1993). A collection of short stories, *Fifth Sunday,* appeared in 1985 and a novel, *Through the Ivory Gate,* was published in 1992 by Pantheon Books. Ms. Dove's most recent book is a verse drama entitled *The Darker Face of Earth* (Story Line Press). A recipient of Fulbright and Guggenheim Fellowships, two National Endowment for the Arts grants, the Academy of American Poets' Lavan Award and the General Electric Foundation Award, Ms. Dove teaches creative writing at the University of Virginia.

SUZANNE J. DOYLE'S

third book of verse, *Dangerous Beauties,* appeared in 1992 from the Marjorie Cantor Press. She lives in the San Francisco Bay area where she is a partner in High*Low Communications, an advertising agency.

RHINA P. ESPAILLAT

has published nearly three hundred poems in journals, including *Poetry, Amelia, Sparrow,* and *Plains Poetry Journal* as well as in anthologies, including *Sarah's Daughters Sing: A Sampler of Poems by Jewish Women* and *In Other Words: Literature by Latinas of the United States* (Arte Publico Press, 1994). Among other awards, she has twice won the Gustav Davidson Memorial Award from the Poetry Society of America. *Lapsing to Grace,* a collection of her poetry with her own illustrations, appeared in 1992 from Bennett and Kitchell.

JULIE FAY

was born in 1951 in Baltimore and grew up on both the West and East coasts. She has published two books of poetry, *In Every Mirror* with Owl Creek Press in 1985 and *Portraits of Women* with Ahsahta Press in 1991. She is currently working on a novel set in 17th-century America, based on the life of Hannah Dustin.

ANNIE FINCH

was educated at Yale University, Stanford University, and the graduate creative writing program at the University of Houston. Her manuscript of poems, "Chain of Women," won the 1993 Nicholas Roerich fellowship. She is also the author of the book-length poem *The Encyclopedia of Scotland* (1982) and of a critical study, *The Ghost of Meter: Culture and Prosody in American Free Verse* (University of Michigan Press, 1993). She is currently Poet-in-Residence and Director of Creative Writing at the University of Northern Iowa, where she edits *Poems & Poetics.*

JOAN AUSTIN GEIER'S

poetry collection, *Mother of Tribes* (Four Circles Press), was published in 1987 and her children's book, *Garbage Can Cat,* has sold over a half-million copies. Her poetry, fiction and non-fiction for children and adults have appeared in numerous publications, including *Good Housekeeping* and *The Christian Science Monitor.*

SARAH GORHAM

is the author of two collections of poetry, *Don't Go Back to Sleep* (1989) and *The Night Lifted Us* (Larkspur Press, 1991). Other work has appeared in national magazines including *Grand Street, Poetry, Kenyon Review, Antæus,* and *Ploughshares,* as well as in two anthologies: *Love Poems by Women* and *Contemporary New England Poetry: A Sampler.* She was a 1990 winner of the Carolyn Kizer award from *Poetry Northwest,* a 1983 winner of the PSA Gertrude Claytor Prize, and a recipient of many fellowships. An Artist-in-Residence since 1992, she has taught at elementary schools throughout Kentucky.

JANE GREER

has edited and published *Plains Poetry Journal* since 1981. She is the author of *Bathsheba on the Third Day* (The Cummington Press [Omaha], 1986). She lives in North Dakota where she is public information director for the Department of Transportation and is active with fetal alcohol syndrome and right-to-life organizations.

EMILY GROSHOLZ

is the author of three books of poetry: *Eden* (Johns Hopkins, 1992); *Shores and Headlands* (Princeton, 1988); and *The River Painter* (U. of Illinois, 1984). She teaches philosophy at Pennsylvania State University.

MARILYN HACKER

is the author of seven books of poetry, including *Going Back to the River* (Random House, 1990), the verse novel *Love, Death, and the Changing of the Seasons* (Arbor House/William Morrow, 1986), and *The Hang-Glider's Daughter,* published in London by Onlywomen Press in 1990. She received the National Book Award in 1975 for *Presentation Piece,* which was also a Lamont Poetry Selection of the Academy of American Poets. Active in the women's and lesbian movements since 1976, she was for four years the editor of the feminist literary magazine *13th Moon.* She is presently editor of the *Kenyon Review,* bringing a multicultural and feminist viewpoint to one of the United States' most "august" literary magazines. *Against Silence: New and Selected Poems* will be published by Copper Canyon in the summer of 1994.

RACHEL HADAS

is professor of English at the Newark campus of Rutgers University. The most recent of her many books are *Unending Dialogue: Voices From an AIDS Poetry Workshop* (Faber & Faber, 1991) and *Mirrors of Astonishment* (Rutgers University Press, 1992).

JOSEPHINE JACOBSEN

was born in Ontario, Canada in 1908. She is the author of many books of poetry, including *The Chinese Insomniacs* (1981), *The Sisters*, and *Distances* (1991). In 1971, she was appointed Poetry Consultant for the Library of Congress. She has been a frequent recipient of grants from the MacDowell Colony and from Yaddo, and has received awards from the American Academy of Arts and Letters (1982), the Poetry Society of America (1993), and the Academy of American Poets (1989).

LENORE KEESHIG-TOBIAS

was born on the Cape Croker Reserve in Ontario and currently lives in Toronto. She is a single mother of three daughters, a Native American activist, and an editor for *Sweetgrass*. "Mother and Child" first appeared in the anthology *A Gathering of Spirit: Writing and Art by North American Indian Women*, edited by Beth Brant (Rockland, Maine: Sinister Wisdom Books, 1984).

DOLORES KENDRICK

is the author of three books of poetry, most recently *The Women of Plums: Poems in the Voices of Slave Women* (William Morrow, 1989), which received the Anisfield-Wolf Award in 1990, was named the New York Public Library's Best Book

DOLORES KENDRICK (CON'T.)

for Teenagers in 1991, and which has recently been adapted for the stage. Her two earlier books are *Through the Ceiling,* originally published in London as part of the famed Heritage poetry series, and *Now is the Thing to Praise.* Her work has also been translated into Chinese and published in the Shangdon Province, Mainland China. Recipient of a Fulbright Award, two Yaddo fellowships, and a National Endowment for the Arts award, she lives in Washington, D.C. and is Vira I. Heinz Professor Emerita of Phillips Exeter Academy.

JANE KENYON'S

fourth book of poems, *Constance,* was published last year by Graywolf Press. Her work appears frequently in magazines, and she has held fellowships from the National Endowment for the Arts and the Guggenheim Foundation.

MARY KINZIE

has published four books of poetry, most recently *Autumn Eros* (Knopf), and a volume of essays, *The Cure of Poetry in an Age of Prose: Moral Essays on the Poet's Calling* (University of Chicago). She has won many awards from such organizations as the Illinois Arts Council, the Guggenheim foundation, and the Poetry Society of America. Since 1975 she has taught at Northwestern University.

CAROLYN KIZER

is the author of numerous books of poetry including *The Ungrateful Garden, Knock Upon Silence, The Nearness of You, Midnight Was My Cry: New and Selected Poems, Mermaids in the Basement,* and *Yin* (BOA Editions, 1984), which won the Pulitzer Prize. She has been poet-in-residence at Columbia, Stanford, Princeton, and the University of Arizona, among others. She has also published translations of poetry from Asian languages. She was the founding editor of *Poetry Northwest* and has most recently published a book of essays, *Proses: On Poems and Poets* with Copper Canyon Press.

PHYLLIS KOESTENBAUM'S

books include *oh I can't she says*, one of the *Library Journal's* "Best Small Press Titles of 1981," and *That Nakedness* (Jungle Garden Press, 1982). She has published widely and was included in the *Best American Poetry* anthologies for 1992 and 1993. An Affiliated Scholar at Stanford University's Institute for Research on Women and Gender, she has completed two sonnet manuscripts, "Criminal Sonnets" and "Scene of the Crime."

SYBIL KOLLAR'S

poetry and fiction have apperared in *The American Voice, Chelsea, 13th Moon* and elsewhere. She is a recipient of many awards including a New York Foundation for the Arts Fellowship in poetry and the Chester H. Jones Foundation's National Poetry Competition award. Recently, she has written poems as text for a song cycle for mezzo-soprano and flute, "Just Us," by Donna Kelly Eastman, which has been performed in Baltimore and Washington.

MAXINE KUMIN

has written ten books of poetry, including *Our Ground Time Here Will Be Brief, The Long Approach, Up Country: Poems of New England, New and Selected,* which won the Pulitzer Prize, and *Nurture* (Viking, 1989). Her book of essays and interviews, *To Make a Prairie,* appeared in the *Poets on Poetry* series from the University of Michigan Press. She has won many awards, has published children's books as well as novels, and was the Consultant in Poetry to the Library of Congress in 1981-82.

PHILLIS LEVIN

is the author of *Temples and Fields* (University of Georgia Press, 1988) which won the Poetry Society of America's Norma Farber First Book Award. Her second book of poems is now in circulation. She is the Senior Editor of *Boulevard* and an Assistant Professor of English and Creative Writing at the University of Maryland at College Park.

JANET LEWIS

has written novels, short stories, children's fiction, songs, lyrics and libretti as well as poetry. Her books of poetry include *The Indians in the Woods, The Wheel in Midsummer, The Earth-Bound, Poems 1924-1944, Poems Old and New*, and *Late Offerings* (Robert L. Barth, 1988).

VASSAR MILLER

is the author of several books of poems including *Adam's Footprint, Struggling to Swim on Concrete*, and most recently *If I Had Wheels or Love: Collected Poems* (SMU Press). She lives in Houston.

LESLIE MONSOUR

was born in Los Angeles, but grew up in Mexico and Panama. Her poetry has appeared in many journals in the U.S. and abroad and in her book *Gringuita Poems* (Missing Measures Press, 1990), as well as on the busses of the city of Santa Monica. Her awards include the T.S. Eliot chapbook award, the John Deupree Award to the Frost Place, and an award from the Pennsylvania Poetry Society. She has been a bilingual poetry instructor in inner city schools and with the U.C.L.A. Extension Writers' Program.

HONOR MOORE'S

book of poems, *Memoir*, was published in 1988 by Chicory Blue Press. Her verse play *Mourning Pictures* was produced on Broadway in 1974, and she is the editor of *The New Women's Theatre: Ten Plays by Contemporary Women*. Currently she is completing a biography of her grandmother, the painter Margarett Sargent, which will be published in 1995.

SUZANNE NOGUERE

is the author of a chapbook, *Hands* (Prairie Flower Press), and of two children's books, *Little Koala* and *Little Raccoon*. She works as the classified ad manager of Printing News/East in New York City. In the last few years she has won the Gertrude B. Claytor Award of the Poetry Society of America and has been a finalist in the National Poetry Series. Her work has appeared in many periodicals including *The Nation* and *Poetry*.

ELISE PASCHEN

graduated from Harvard University in 1982; there she was awarded the Lloyd McKim Garrison Medal for poetry and the Joan Grey Untermyer Poetry Prize. She received her M. Phil. (1984) and D. Phil. (1988) degrees in English Literature from Oxford University. In 1985 the Sycamore Press, Oxford, published a chapbook of her poetry entitled *Houses: Coasts*. Her poems have appeared in *Poetry, The Nation, Western Humanities Review, Poetry Review* (England), *Poetry Ireland, Oxford Poetry and Oxford Magazine*.

MOLLY PEACOCK

is the author of three books of poems, *And Live Apart, Raw Heaven*, and most recently *Take Heart* (Random House, 1989). Among her grants and awards are a National Endowment for the Arts fellowship, two fellowships from the Ingram Merrill Foundation, and three from New York Foundation for the Arts. She has been a visiting professor at a number of universities, including NYU, Barnard, Columbia, Sarah Lawrence and Bucknell. She lives in New York City and in London, Ontario, serves as President of the Poetry Society of America, and works as a free-lance poetry consultant with individual writers and writing programs.

HELEN PINKERTON

is the author of three books of poetry, including *Poems 1946-1976*, as well as many scholarly essays and a critical study, *Melville's Confidence Men and American Politics in the 1850's*. She has held fellowships to the Djerassi Foundation and a Stegner Creative Writing Fellowship at Stanford University. She is currently working on a project called "An Art of Poetry for the 21st Century: A Study of Poetic Form From the Greeks to the Present." The poems included here are part of a sequence called *"The Harvesters" and Other Poems on Works of Art* (R.L. Barth, 1984).

MARY JO SALTER

has published three books of poetry, *Henry Purcell in Japan*, *Unfinished Painting*, and most recently *Sunday Skaters* (Knopf, 1994). She has also published *The Moon Comes Home*, a book for children. A lecturer at Mt. Holyoke, she has won numerous awards including the Lamont Prize, the Witter Bynner Award, the Peter I. B. Lavan Award, and grants from the National Endowment for the Arts, the Ingram Merrill Foundation, and the Guggenheim Foundation. She serves as poetry editor of *The New Republic*.

SONIA SANCHEZ'S

eleven books include *A Blues Book for Blue Black Magical Women*, *I've Been a Woman: New and Selected Poems*, *homegirls & handgrenades*, and *Under a Soprano Sky* (Africa World Press, 1990). She is a contributing editor to *Black Scholar* and has edited two anthologies: *We Be Word Sorcerers: 25 Stories by Black Women* and *360 Degrees of Blackness Coming at You*. She has won a grant from the National Endowment for the Arts and the Lucretia Mott Award, lectures widely, and is currently an Associate Professor at Temple University.

MAY SARTON

has published eighteen books of poetry, including *Collected Poems 1930-1973*, *Letters from Maine: New Poems*, and most recently *The Silence Now: New and Uncollected Earlier Poems* (Norton, 1988). She has also published nineteen novels, including *Joanna and Ulysses* and *Mrs. Stevens Hears the Mermaids Singing*, several plays; and nine books of nonfiction, including several memoirs and journals. The subject of the film *World of Light: A Portrait of May Sarton*, she lives and writes on the coast of Maine.

MAUREEN SEATON

has published poetry in magazines including *Chelsea, Massachusetts Review, Southern Poetry Review*, and *New Letters*. Her poetry collection, *Fear of Subways*, was published by Eighth Mountain Press in 1991 and includes thirty-two sonnets.

LESLIE SIMON

has taught in the Poetics Program of New College of California and in the Women's Studies Program at San Francisco State University. She currently teaches at City College of San Francisco. Her most recent of several collections of poems is *Collisions and Transformations* (Coffee House Press).

ELIZABETH SPIRES

is the author of three collections of poetry: *Globe, Swan's Island*, and most recently *Annonciade* (Viking Penguin, 1989). Her work has been featured in *The Morrow Anthology of Younger American Poets, The Direction of Poetry*, and the last four editions of *The Best American Poetry*. A recent Guggenheim fellow, she lives in Baltimore and teaches at Goucher College and in the Writing Seminars at Johns Hopkins.

MAURA STANTON

won the Yale Series of Younger Poets prize in 1975 with her first book of poetry, *Snow on Snow*. Since then she has published two volumes of poems, *Cries of Swimmers* (Utah, 1982) and *Tales of the Supernatural* (Godine, 1988). Her fourth book of poetry, *Life Among the Trolls*, is forthcoming from Godine. She teaches at Indiana University.

PATRICIA STORACE

is a poet and essayist and has served as poetry editor of *The Paris Review*. Her poems have appeared in *Parnassus, Harper's, The New York Review of Books*, and elsewhere, and her first book of poems, *Heredities* (Beacon, 1987) was published in the Barnard New Women Poets Series. She is currently working on a travel book about Greece and a collection of poems.

MONA VAN DUYN

was Poet Laureate of the United States in 1992-93. She has published nine books of poetry including *To See, To Take, Merciful Disguises*, and most recently *Firefall* and *If It Be Not I: Collected Poems 1959-1982* (Knopf, 1993). Awards she has received include the National Book Award, the Bollingen Prize, the Ruth Lilly Award from *Poetry*, and the Shelley Memorial Prize from the Poetry Society of America, as well as Guggenheim and National Endowment for the Arts grants. She is a Chancellor of the Academy of American Poets.

ALMA LUZ VILLANUEVA'S

books of poetry include *Bloodroot, Mother, May I?, La Chingada, Life Span,* and *Planet.* Her work has been anthologized in *Women Poets of the World, She Rises Like the Sun, Latino Poets in the Nineties,* and other collections. Her first novel, *The Ultraviolet Sky,* won the Amercian Book Award in 1989 and was chosen for *New American Writing, 1990.* She teaches creative writing at the University of California at Santa Cruz.

ANNE WALDMAN

is the author of thirty books of poetry, including *Helping the Dreamer: New and Selected Poems 1966-1988* (Coffee House Press) and *Iovis,* a book-length poem, as well as numerous translations, essays, and reviews in publications ranging from *Poetry, The Paris Review,* and *American Poetry Review* to *The New York Times Book Review, Newsweek, Vogue, Glamour, Tricycle,* and *Rolling Stone.* She has performed her work on recordings, films, videos, radio and television programs, including a tour with Bob Dylan's Rolling Thunder Review. Her reading tours have included the U.S., Italy, India, Central America, and the U.K. She was for many years director of the Poetry Project of St. Mark's Church in New York City, and is currently director of the Jack Kerouac School of Disembodied Poetics at the Naropa Institute in Boulder, Colorado.

Marilyn Nelson Waniek

graduated from the University of California, Davis and holds postgraduate degrees from the University of Pennsylvania (M.A.) and the University of Minnesota (Ph.D.). Her books are *For the Body* (1978), *Mama's Promises* (1985), and *The Homeplace* (1990), all published by L.S.U. Press, and two collections of verse for children. A new collection, *Magnificat*, is forthcoming from L.S.U. Press. She has received many awards for her work and is a professor of English at the University of Connecticut, Storrs.

Kathleene West

is the author of six books of poetry, most recently *Water Witching* (Copper Canyon Press, 1984) and *The Farmer's Daughter* (Sandhills Press, 1990). She was a Fulbright Scholar to Iceland and has travelled widely, most recently to Southeast Asia. An Associate Professor of English at New Mexico State University, she serves as alternating poetry editor of *Puerto del Sol*.

Mildred Weston

was born in Waterville, Washington and has lived in Spokane since the age of four. She has published two books of poetry, *Individual Weather* and *The Green Dusk: Selected Poems* (Owl Creek Press, 1987), as well as a biographical study, *Vachel Lindsay: Poet in Exile*.

Gail White

has published several chapbooks, including *Sibyl and Sphinx* (Rockhill Press, 1988) and *All Night in the Churchyard* (Proof-Rock, 1986). She is the founding editor of the *Piedmont Literary Review*.

Carolyn Beard Whitlow

is Associate Professor of English at Guilford College in Greensboro, North Carolina, where she teaches African-American literature and creative writing. She completed an M.F.A. at

CAROLYN BEARD WHITLOW (CON'T.)

Brown University in 1984 and her first collection of poetry, *Wild Meat* (Lost Roads Press) appeared in 1986. Her poems have been published in *The Massachusetts Review, Kenyon Review, Indiana Review, Callaloo, 13th Moon, Northeast Journal,* and elsewhere.

NANCY WILLARD'S

books include seven books of poetry, most recently *Household Tales of Moon and Water* and *Water Walker* (Knopf); two novels, *Things Invisible to See* and *Sister Water* (Knopf); many books for children including *Pish Posh, Hieronymus Bosch* and *A Visit to William Blake's Inn: Poems for Innocent and Experienced Travelers* (Harcourt Brace); and *A Nancy Willard Reader* (University Press of New England).

NELLIE WONG

is the author of two collections of poetry, *Dreams in Harrison Railroad Park* and *The Death of Long Steam Lady* (West End Press, 1986). She travelled to China in 1983 with the first American Women Writers Tour hosted by the Chinese Writers Association and has received a Woman of Words award from the Women's Foundation. Her poetry has appeared in numerous anthologies and journals including *This Bridge Called My Back: Writings by Radical Women of Color, The Forbidden Stitch,* and *Dissident Song,* and her work is co-featured in the documentary, *Mitsuye and Nellie, Asian American Poets.*

CELESTE TURNER WRIGHT

is a Professor of English, Emerita, at the University of California, Davis, where she was chair of her department for twenty-seven years and taught for fifty-one years. She has published three collections of poetry, *Etruscan Princess, Seasoned Timber,* and *A Sense of Place* (winner of a Silver Medal from the Commonwealth Club in 1973) as well as a memoir, *University Woman.* She is currently preparing her *Collected Poems: 1924-1984* for publication.

TOMMA MAAS

Editor and poet Annie Finch was educated at Yale University, the University of Houston Creative Writing Program, and Stanford University. She is the author of *The Encyclopedia of Scotland* (1982), a book-length poem, and of *The Ghost of Meter: Culture and Prosody in American Free Verse* (1993). She is currently Poet-in-Residence and Assistant Professor of English at the University of Northern Iowa, where she edits the journal *Poems & Poetics*.

THE TYPE IS PALATINO
COVER PAINTING BY ALIX BAER
BOOK DESIGN BY LYSA M^cDOWELL
PRINTING BY DATA REPRODUCTIONS CORPORATION